William Dillon

The Dismal Science

A Criticism on Modern English Political Economy

William Dillon

The Dismal Science
A Criticism on Modern English Political Economy

ISBN/EAN: 9783744645461

Printed in Europe, USA, Canada, Australia, Japan

Cover: Foto ©Suzi / pixelio.de

More available books at **www.hansebooks.com**

" THIS great law rules all the wide design : that success (while society is guided by laws of competition) signifies always so much victory over your neighbour as to obtain the direction of his work, and to take the profits of it."— JOHN RUSKIN.

THE

DISMAL SCIENCE

A CRITICISM

ON

𝕸𝖔𝖉𝖊𝖗𝖓 𝕰𝖓𝖌𝖑𝖎𝖘𝖍 𝕻𝖔𝖑𝖎𝖙𝖎𝖈𝖆𝖑 𝕰𝖈𝖔𝖓𝖔𝖒𝖞.

BY

WILLIAM DILLON,

OF THE IRISH BAR, AND OF THE AMERICAN BAR (STATE OF ILLINOIS),
MEMBER OF THE ROYAL IRISH ACADEMY.

DUBLIN

M. H. GILL & SON, 50 UPPER SACKVILLE STREET
LONDON : SIMPKIN, MARSHALL & CO., STATIONERS' HALL COURT.

1882

PRINTED BY M. H. GILL AND SON, 50 UPPER SACKVILLE-STREET, DUBLIN.

PREFACE.

———◆———

ABSTRACT Political Economy is by no means an
inviting study. If we except the "Wealth of
Nations," the works of the leading Economists of
the English school are the driest of dry reading.
But the subject of which Political Economy treats
is one in which most men take a keen interest;
and if it were only certain that the teaching was
sound and useful, few would regard the time and
trouble spent in mastering it as thrown away. Is
the teaching sound and useful? This is a question
about which there has been much difference of
opinion, more especially of late years. The estimate which the student will ultimately form of the
value of the teaching will, I think, depend a good
deal upon the spirit in which he approaches the
study. If his desire be simply to read some one
standard text-book on the Current Political Economy with the object of being able to discourse

learnedly about land, labour, and capital, it is quite
possible that he may close the book with the
impression that he has learned something very
useful, and is a much wiser man than when he
opened it. If, however, his object be to get to the
bottom of the matter, and, so far as he may be
able, to understand and master all that modern
Political Economy has to teach him, the result will
probably be somewhat different. The mental course
of a student of the latter class will, I venture to
think, be somewhat as follows.

In the first work on the " Principles of Political
Economy" which he may read, he will find some
doctrines which he cannot very clearly understand,
and many which seem to be of an extremely
abstract nature, and very far removed from the
realities of things. Probably, however, he will
postpone criticism and dissent until he has gone
deeper into the study, hoping that wider reading
may clear up much that at first sight looks perplexing. When, in following out this policy, he has
read the works of three or four leading Economists,
his doubts and difficulties, so far from being cleared
away, will be decidedly increased. He will be

astonished to find that, after a century of active
discussion, the widest differences of opinion still
prevail amongst the teachers as to some of the
most important questions in their so-called science.
In this way his faith in the teachers will naturally
be shaken, and he will be led to examine for himself the soundness of the doctrines. This examination will most probably enable him to see why it
is that Political Economy has at present such very
slight authority with practical statesmen. Finally,
he will be anxious to know in what way the errors
and shortcomings which he thinks he can detect in
the teachings of the Economists are to be accounted
for. This will naturally lead him to examine the
method of inquiry by which the conclusions have
been arrived at.

The foregoing brief sketch of the experiences of
an imaginary student will suggest the course pursued in the following criticism. In the first, or
introductory, chapter opinions are cited and facts
adduced tending to show that of late years Political
Economy has been losing ground in the public
estimation, and that at present its authority in
practical politics is at a very low ebb. Some

general objections, having reference to the subject-
matter of the science and the dismal character of
its teachings, are also considered in this chapter.
In the second chapter the subject of differences of
opinion is dealt with. Some questions of the first
importance are selected, and the teachings of divers
eminent authorities upon these questions are briefly
examined.   In the third chapter some remarks are
made upon a defect in the Current Political Economy which is at once a cause, and to some extent
a particular example, of the differences of opinion
previously commented on.   These second and third
chapters are necessarily, in a great degree, mere
compilations. They may with advantage be skipped
by any reader who is willing to accept on trust the
statements (1) that the differences of opinion
amongst the Economists on questions of the first
importance are such that the student who is anxious
merely to learn and not to criticise finds it impossible to know what to believe and what not to
believe ; and (2) that several of the leading terms
of the so-called science are used in different
senses not only by different writers, but frequently by the same writer. We next reach the

critical stage, properly so called, the first phase of which may be termed the stage of criticism as regards the teachings. In the fourth and fifth chapters two subjects of the first importance—the causes which determine the rate of wages, and the principles which should regulate international trade—are selected, and the teachings of the Current Economy in reference to these subjects are examined somewhat in detail. Lastly, we reach the stage of criticism as regards the method. In the final chapter some remarks are made in reference to the method of inquiry pursued by the English school of Economists. The objections to which that method is liable are briefly dwelt on, and the course is indicated which, in the opinion of the present writer, the new departure ought to take. This part of the inquiry is dealt with in a very cursory and superficial manner. The reader who may care to pursue the subject for himself, will find it more fully, and, I need hardly add, more ably discussed in the tenth, eleventh, fourteenth, and twenty-sixth of Professor Cliffe Leslie's " Essays in Political and Moral Philosophy," in an Essay on " The present Position and Prospects of Political

Economy," by Dr. Ingram of Trinity College, Dublin, and in the fourth chapter of Mr. H. M. Posnett's recently published book on the Historical Method.

According to the learned author of " What Science is saying about Ireland," the Celts are prognathous. It is, no doubt, in the highest degree presumptuous for an individual belonging to a prognathous race to dare to criticise doctrines propounded by eminent Englishmen. I am painfully conscious of the presumption. Should the following criticism chance to attract the notice of those persons of a higher order of intellect, known as English Political Economists, I cannot reasonably expect that it will excite any feelings other than those of anger or contempt. In the third chapter of " Theophrastus Such," George Eliot has given us an amusing sketch of the fate which the unfortunate Merman brought upon himself by his rash criticisms of the orthodox doctrines regarding the Magicodumbras, and the Zuzumotzis. The criticisms might or might not be sound; but the first object of Grampus and his friends naturally and properly was to extinguish Merman. This primary object having been once accomplished, they were then in a position to assimilate at their leisure such of his criticisms as might prove well founded. If this was the fate of a member of the superior race, what result might have been looked for had Merman been a prognathous Celt?

But the Professors of the Dismal Science are by no means the only persons whom it deeply concerns to know whether the teachings of the Current Political Economy are true or false. There are numbers of English-speaking people in all parts of the world who feel in their hearts the need of true and sufficient answers to certain great social problems; and who, at the same time feel, in an instinctive sort of way, that the answers given by English Political Economists are not what they need. To examine carefully into this feeling of distrust, so as to ascertain in how far it is well grounded, demands an amount of study and thought, and therefore of time, which many people cannot afford to give. To these last it is hoped that this book may afford some little help.

It is, no doubt, much easier to find fault with the doctrines of others than to discern and teach the true doctrine. The latter kind of work will always and justly rank far above the former. But the work of the fault-finder, lower in kind though it be, is often very useful in preparing the way for the teacher. When the field is covered with weeds and briars, some preliminary work is needed before the seed can be sown and the harvest reaped. For a long time, the field of Political Economy was neglected, or at best cultivated upon a wrong system, and the result has been a very luxuriant growth of weeds. To clear away these weeds is a necessary, if an irksome task. Some good work of this kind has been done of late years ; but even in this lower department much remains to do. Some day or other, let us hope, a great, original thinker will take up the nobler work where Adam Smith left it, more than a hundred years ago, and carry it on towards the harvest. Meantime, those who are neither great nor original must only be content to lend such aid as they are able in the humbler work of clearing the ground.

WILLIAM DILLON.

2 *North Great George's-street,*
Dublin, May, 1882.

the true doctrine. The latter kind of work will
always and justly rank far above the former. But
the work of the fault-finder, lower in kind though
it be, is often very useful in preparing the way for

WILLIAM DILLON.

*2 North Great George's-street,
Dublin, May,* 1882.

EDITIONS AND ABBREVIATIONS.

In this book the following abbreviations are used in citing the works most frequently referred to.

1. Principles &c., by Ricardo, stands for Principles of Political Economy and Taxation, by David Ricardo, 2nd edition (1819). As regards this and the following abbreviations, it may be as well to observe that the author's name is not always given as part of the reference. Thus, where it is clear from the text that the passage cited is taken from some work of Ricardo's, the reference in the foot-note might be simply "Principles &c.," with the page.

2. Principles &c., by M'Culloch, stands for Principles of Political Economy, by J. C. M'Culloch, 2nd edition.

3. Principles &c., by Mill, stands for Principles of Political Economy, by John Stuart Mill, People's edition (1878).

4. Essay &c., by Malthus, stands for Essay on the Principle of Population, by the Rev. T. R. Malthus, 7th edition (1872).

5. Character &c., by Professor Cairnes, stands for Character and Logical Method of Political Economy, by J. E. Cairnes, 2nd edition (1875).

6. Some leading Principles &c., by Professor Cairnes, stands for Some Leading Principles of Political Economy newly expounded, by J. E. Cairnes (1874).

7. Theory &c., by Professor Jevons, stands for Theory of Political Economy, by W. Stanley Jevons (1871).

8. Manual &c., by Professor Fawcett, stands for Manual of Political Economy, by Henry Fawcett, 4th edition.

9. Chapters &c., by Professor Price, stands for Chapters on Practical Economy, by Bonamy Price (1878).

10. Social Science &c., by Professor Thompson, stands for Social Science and National Economy, by Robert Ellis Thompson of the University of Pennsylvania, Philadelphia (1875).

11. Present Position &c., by Dr. Ingram, stands for The Present Position and Prospects of Political Economy, being the Introductory Address delivered in the Section of Economic Science and Statistics of the British Association at its meeting in Dublin, in 1878, by John K. Ingram.

12. Essays &c., by Professor Leslie, stands for Essays on Political and Moral Philosophy, by T. E. Cliffe Leslie, Dublin (1879).

13. Principles &c., by Professor Roscher, stands for Principles of Political Economy, by William Roscher, of the University of Leipzig, translated from the 13th German edition, by John J. Lalor, Chicago (1878).

CONTENTS.

THE DISMAL SCIENCE.

CHAPTER I.

Present Position of the Science.

"Respectable Professors of the Dismal Science, soft you a little. For my sins, I have read much in those inimitable volumes of yours— really, I should think, some barrowfuls of them in my time—and in these last forty years of theory and practice, have pretty well seized what of Divine Message you were sent with to me. Perhaps as small a message, give me leave to say, as ever there was such a noise made about before. . . . . Professors of the Dismal Science, I perceive that the length of your tether is now pretty well run, and that I must request you to talk a little lower in future."—CARLYLE, *Latter-Day Pamphlets.*

MR. CARLYLE was, I believe, the first to bestow upon Political Economy the nickname of the "Dismal Science." It is not always easy to satisfactorily explain the Carlylean phraseology ; but in the present case the reason for the name is sufficiently obvious. We may safely assume that the adjective "dismal" was principally suggested by the gloomy outlook for

2

L u

the future of humanity, presented to us in the teachings of the current English Economy upon the subjects of population and wages. But if we want to know how it is that a nickname comes to be a popular favourite, we must often look for reasons other than those which may have induced the author of the name to bestow it. It is probable that only a small percentage of those who speak of Political Economy as the " Dismal Science " have ever troubled their heads to understand the bearings upon the future of the human race of the Malthusian law of population, taken in connection with the doctrine that wages come from capital. The generality of men—even the generality of intelligent and fairly educated men—dislike and distrust Political Economy. With much the greater number the Carlylean nickname serves as a convenient form of expressing a somewhat vague and indefinite sentiment. Political Economy is dry and dull reading, abstract, non-practical; therefore, it may be described in a comprehensive and general way as " dismal."

" Professors of the Dismal Science, I perceive that the length of your tether is now pretty well run, and that I must request of you to talk a little lower in future." It was hardly to be expected that the Professors here addressed would at once strike their colours in obedience to this summons. Some of them may have felt in their hearts a suspicion that the attack made upon them was not wholly without good grounds. Others honestly resented this and similar attacks upon their science as being the outcome of prejudice and ignorance. There are still numbers of able and sincere men in England whose faith in the teachings of Political Economy is unshaken ; men who believe that the so-called deductive science, first elaborated by Ricardo, and subsequently developed and expounded by Senior, Mill, and Cairnes, is, in the main, a safe guide for the practical statesman. But, however great may be the difference of opinion as to the amount of authority which Political Economy *ought* to exercise in practical politics, there can, I apprehend, be little room for difference of opinion as to the amount of authority which it actually *does* exercise.

The passage quoted at the head of the chapter was written as far back as 1850. It certainly cannot be said that since then the influence and authority of Political Economy have increased. Whatever movement has taken place has been distinctly a retrograde movement. It would be hardly too much to say that at no time during the last hundred years has the authority of Political Economy in practical politics been at a lower ebb than at present.

It is only fair to the "Professors of the Dismal Science" to say that if they have not admitted that their science is in itself dismal, they have at least admitted that in many respects it is in a very dismal condition. In the year 1876 a dinner was given by the Political Economy Club to celebrate the hundredth anniversary of the publication of the "Wealth of Nations." The chair was occupied by Mr. Gladstone, and the principal speaker was Mr. Lowe (now Lord Sherbrooke). The question propounded for discussion was—"What are the more important results which have followed from the publication of the 'Wealth of Nations,' just one hundred years ago; and in what principal directions do the doctrines of that book still remain to be applied?" The speech of Mr. Lowe, in opening the discussion, was despondent in so far as regards the second part of the question. He held that Political Economy had done great things, but that it was not likely to accomplish much more. "The great work has been done," said Mr. Lowe. Upon the whole, it would seem that Mr. Gladstone was substantially accurate when he observed, at a later stage of the discussion, that Mr. Lowe had "taken what some might think a desponding view of the functions of the science of Political Economy in the future." So, again, other members of the Club expressed grave apprehension and regret at the tendency of recent legislation to disregard the cardinal principle of English Political Economy—the principle of *laissez faire*. But, perhaps, the most striking testimony furnished by Economists themselves to the decline in the authority of their science is that to be found in a speech delivered by Mr. Goschen in the House of Commons on June 29th, 1877. I believe I am justified in classing

Mr. Goschen as a distinguished Political Economist; and certainly, in the speech I am referring to, he distinctly asserts his faith in the principles of the Current Economy. The latter portion of the speech is one long lament over the miserable condition to which Political Economy had come. " Political Economy," said Mr. Goschen, "has been dethroned in this House, and philanthropy has been allowed to take its place." And, again, " Political Economy was the bugbear of the working classes, and philanthropy, he was sorry to say, was their idol. . . . . He believed that there was danger of the principles of Political Economy being more and more disregarded ; they were more and more disregarded in that House."* Professor Bonamy Price, in the first chapter of his " Practical Economy," testifies to a like effect.

But, if we turn from the lamentations of Economists to examine the recent tendency of legislation in various countries, we find even stronger evidence of the decline in the authority of Political Economy. The cardinal principle of the English school of Economists is, as we have said, the principle of *laissez faire*. The chief applications of this principle in practice may be classed under two great heads, namely, Free Contract and Free Trade. In 1860, an Act was passed amending the Land Laws of Ireland, with the object of promoting more perfect freedom of contract. In 1870, an Act was passed taking a decided step in the oppo-

* See Hansard, vol. iv. for 1877, pp. 564-566.

site direction. In 1881, an Act was passed by which the policy of the Act of 1860 was entirely reversed, and freedom of contract, so far as concerns the letting of agricultural land in Ireland, was practically put an end to. I am not concerned here to express any opinion as to whether or not the special circumstances of Ireland were of a kind to render necessary some such legislation. I merely wish to point out that a law which imposes on the State the duty of supervising all contracts between landlord and tenant is a tremendous experiment, and an experiment which sets the fundamental principles of the current Political Economy completely at defiance. In England, too, the Factory Acts, and the Acts limiting the hours of labour, are distinct departures from the principle that free contract and free competition may safely be left to settle the relations of master and servant. And obviously when once this principle is departed from, it is impossible to say where the line may be drawn, or how far the legislature may deem it expedient to go in the direction of protecting the labourer against the so-called tyranny of capital. In America the principle of protecting the labourer against the capitalist has received a new development. Apparently the legislators at Washington are at last coming round to the views advocated with such force by one of the leading characters in Mr. Bret Harte's immortal poem. "We are ruined by Chinese cheap labour," would seem to have been the motto upon which the

Foreign Committee of the Senate acted when they recently recommended the legislature to "go for that heathen Chinee." Again, if we look at the chief progressive countries of the world, excepting England, we see that of late years the principle of Free Trade has decidedly been losing rather than gaining ground. In the United States, for the last twenty years, the tariff has been strictly protective. Germany, after trying the experiment of a moderate tariff for some ten or fifteen years, has in 1879 re-imposed duties which are practically protective. We all know what has recently happened in the case of France. The treaty of 1860 was a triumph for the doctrines of the English Economists, in so far as a commercial treaty between two nations, based upon the principle of reciprocity, can be said to be a step in the direction of Free Trade. But it would seem that the present French Government are not willing to maintain even this slight concession, but prefer to return to the state of things which existed before the treaty. If, then, we take the four most powerful, best educated, and most progressive nations of the world, England, the United States, France, and Germany, we find that in three out of the four the tendency of recent legislation has been to set at defiance the principle which is re-garded by all English Economists of eminence as one of the most important and one of the least question-able of the teachings of their science. In England the leading statesmen have, until recently, been in

entire accord with the Political Economists upon this
question of Free Trade.   But of late the Conservative
leaders have shown some disposition to coquet with
that form of Protection known as "Fair Trade."
Speaking at Newcastle in last October, the leader of
the Tory party, in his usual incisive and vigorous style,
observed :—"In spite of any formula, in spite of any
cry of Free Trade, if I saw that by raising a duty upon
luxuries, or by threatening to raise it, I could exercise
a pressure upon foreign powers, and induce them to
lower their tariffs, I should pitch orthodoxy and for-
mulas to the winds, and exercise the pressure."   A
still more vigorous and daring, if a less responsible,
statesman on the Tory side, Mr. James Lowther, has
openly declared for the Fair Trade programme.

If we turn to examine the recent course of events
in the British Colonies, we find a like tendency apparent.   The case of Canada is peculiarly significant.
After a long experiment of what was practically Free
Trade, and having had the opportunity of comparing
the effects of this policy with the results achieved by
her next door neighbours under an opposite policy,
Canada two or three years ago has adopted Protection.   Of the present tariff of Canada, Mr. T. H.
Farrer observes that "it is thoroughly protective,
whatever Mr. Goldwin Smith may say to the contrary."   Amongst the Australian colonies, New South
Wales is, and has been, upon the whole, a Free Trade
colony.   In Victoria, the duties, since 1879, at all

events, have been strictly protective. In the other Australian colonies, as well as in the Cape of Good Hope, the tendency of late years has been decidedly towards Protection.* In India the duties have been lowered of late, "but," says Mr. Farrer, "this has been done, not by the people, or even by the Government of India, but by English influence."

We have, then, the admissions of the Economists themselves as well as the evidence of contemporary history to justify the assertion, that never, since some few years after the publication of the "Wealth of Nations," has the unpopularity of Political Economy been more marked or its influence in practical politics at a lower ebb than at the present time. The next question will naturally be—Why is this? To this question the answers of the Professors differ widely. In Germany and in the United States a school of Economists has arisen who hold that the teachers of Political Economy are, to a great extent, themselves to blame for the unpopularity of their science. Ac-

---

* I make this statement on the authority of Mr. Farrer, although I observe a passage in a recent article on "Protection in Young Communities," by Mr. Baden-Powell, which would seem to imply that the fact is otherwise. (See the *Fortnightly Review* for March, 1882, p. 379.)

I may add that several of the statements above made are taken at second hand from Mr. Farrer's recent pamphlet on "Free Trade and Fair Trade" (see chaps. 5 and 6). I have assumed that I am safe in accepting as correct Mr. Farrer's statistics and statements of fact without taking the trouble to verify them.

cording to this school, the deductive method of treating economic problems, which was for the first time rigorously applied by Ricardo, and which has since continued to be the method adopted, with little variation, by the leading English teachers, is radically wrong, and can never lead to anything but a series of abstract theories, having little or no practical bearing upon the actual facts of society. The most distinguished living member of this school in Germany is Professor Roscher, of the University of Leipzig ; in America, Professor Thompson, of the University of Pennsylvania.

The teachers of Political Economy in England have been accustomed to regard and speak of their science as a peculiarly English creation. Hence that disregard of the current of foreign opinion, which is characteristic of Englishmen in general, has been even more than usually marked in the case of the English school of Economists. It was not till long after the new departure had created a school of National Economy in Germany, and had won distinguished converts in the United States, that the English teachers first seemed to become aware of its existence. Professor Cliffe Leslie, whose recent and untimely death every well-wisher to Political Economy must deeply deplore, has of late years signalised himself amongst his fellow-professors as an able and earnest advocate of the new methods. So also Dr. Ingram, of Trinity College, Dublin, in an address delivered before the Economic and Statistical Section of the British Association, in 1878, has pointed out what he conceives to be the leading errors in the method of treatment pursued by the Ricardoan* Economists. Professor Bonamy Price admits the decline in the authority of Political Economy, and he also thinks that the teachers themselves are largely to blame.† But, up to the present, those who admit that the unpopularity of their science‡ is to a great extent deserved form the exception rather than the rule amongst English Economists. Of the living exponents of the science in England probably the two best known are Professor Fawcett (now Postmaster-General) and Professor Stanley Jevons. In the 4th edition of Professor Fawcett's "Manual of Political Economy" the subject is handled strictly upon the lines of the "orthodox" deductive or *a priori* method. Professor Jevons, in his "Theory of Political Economy," attempts to give to the study an even more rigidly scientific form. He regards it as a branch of

---

* I use this adjective to denote the School of Economists founded by Ricardo, and to which nearly all the English teachers who have since expounded the science may be said to belong. J. S. Mill is not so exclusively deductive as the others ; but, in the main, his method is the same as that of Ricardo. When I speak of the "Current Economy,' I mean the same school, unless the context shows that the phrase is used in a wider meaning.

† See Chapters &c., chap 1.

‡ I use this word "science" as being convenient, and hard to replace ; but the reader must not, therefore, conclude that I admit the right of Political Economy to be called a science in the strict sense of the word.

mathematics, and, as such, a strictly deductive science. "There are," he tells us, "a few of the simplest principles or axioms concerning the nature of the human mind," upon which he claims that we can ground "a complete deductive mathematical theory."* He proposes to treat Political Economy as a "calculus of pleasure and pain." Again, in a later work, Professor Jevons is far indeed from admitting that the unpopularity of the science is due to any fault on the part of its teachers. In his "Primer of Political Economy" he observes:—"The fact is that just as physical science was formerly hated, so now there is a kind of ignorant dislike of Political Economy. People wish to follow their own impulses and prejudices, and are vexed when told that they are doing just what will have the opposite effect to that which they intend." This is all very well; but it hardly accounts for the slight authority which Political Economy seems to hold in the estimation of statesmen, many of whom are admittedly familiar with its teachings.

But while we may differ from Professor Jevons and those who think with him in so far as they attribute the unpopularity of Political Economy entirely to the ignorance and prejudice of the public, it would be vain to deny that ignorance and prejudice have a good deal to say to it. We all know how often that most valuable, but much abused faculty, "common sense," is relied on as conclusively disposing of questions with

* Theory &c., pp. 3-6 and 23-24.

which it is wholly incompetent to deal. While the mercantile theory was in vogue, nine men out of ten would have regarded it as "contrary to common sense" to deny that the wealthiest country was the country which had most money in it. I am not even sure that there are not many men to-day whose common sense would tell them the same thing. Again, we are tolerably familiar with the man who delights to call himself "practical," and upon whom a "theoriser" has much the same effect that a red rag is said to have upon a bull. The science of Political Economy, as taught in England to-day, has been elaborated and expounded almost exclusively by theorisers—men who have taken no active part in the practical management of the matters which form the subject of their teaching.* The English are a people gifted with a very large share of common sense, but who carry their belief in the omniscience of common sense to a very absurd degree. It is not to be wondered at that such a people should feel indignant and inclined to rebel when the doctrinaires of Political Economy tell them, in an arrogant and dogmatic fashion, that their favourite methods of doing things are completely mistaken. The truth is that the popular dislike of Political Economy is compounded of two elements— the one rational, the other irrational. To separate the one element from the other so as to determine

* Even the case of Mr. Mill can hardly be said to constitute an exception to this statement.

precisely in how far the popular distrust has valid grounds is not an easy task. In the following pages an attempt will be made to accomplish some small portion of this task. I shall endeavour to state some of the grounds which induce me to hold that the public have a valid cause of complaint against the so-called science of Political Economy as taught in England, and that the teachers of the science must, to a great extent, make a new departure, unless indeed they are content to "talk a little lower in future."

Should any "Professor of the Dismal Science" condescend to read these pages, I can picture to myself the scornful smile which the last paragraph will excite. "So then," he will say, "we are to have some more amateur criticism." One can well sympathise with the Professors of Political Economy in their horror of amateur criticism. Their science has been peculiarly victimised in this way. We have had the vigorous invective which can see in the Current Economy nothing but a series of "prodigious delusions" and "most ludicrous misconceptions," and we have had abundant criticism of a more calm and temperate kind. It is hardly to be expected that fresh criticism of any kind, coming from an amateur, will find much favour with the recognised teachers of the science. There is, however, a good deal to be said in excuse for such criticism. If the recognised teachers of a particular branch of knowledge cannot agree amongst themselves in reference to the most important questions in their science, they can hardly expect the student to agree with everyone of them. He must either give the thing up in despair or make up his mind to differ from some of the authorities. Moreover, several of the most eminent English Political Economists have themselves strongly deprecated the practice of accepting blindly, upon the authority of eminent names, teaching which the student is himself unable to understand or concur in.* When, therefore, Political Economists complain of the surfeit of amateur criticism which has been inflicted upon their science, it seems to me that, in more than one respect, they have themselves to blame.

Political Economy professes to treat of the nature, production, and distribution of wealth. In asserting the right of the branch of knowledge which they profess to rank as a science of the first importance, the teachers of Political Economy have had to contend with two classes of objectors. There are those who, adopting the Pythagorean definition of Philosophy as " the knowledge of immaterial and eternal things," deny that any science dealing merely with material wealth is entitled to a place amongst the highest branches of human knowledge. And there are those who, while fully admitting the importance of the subject matter, deny the truth or the practical utility

* See, for example, some observations on " The Noxious Influence of Authority" at the end of Professor Jevons' " Theory of Political Economy."

of the doctrines propounded in reference thereto. Professor Cairnes refers to the first class of objections as " the various objections of a popular kind, which have been advanced against the study of Political Economy upon the ground, as it has been phrased, of its exclusive devotion to wealth."* It surprises me a little to find so eminent an authority referring to this class of objections as being "of a popular kind." I should rather have thought that the generality of people would not require much argument to convince them of the importance of material wealth. The popular distrust and dislike at present manifested towards Political Economy cannot certainly be said to be due in any appreciable degree to an undervaluing of the subject matter of the science. Objections of this kind come from a very limited class. If I were to assume, without further comment, that " material wealth" is a subject of the first importance, few readers would object that the assumption was unwarranted. But, as I have referred to this class of objections, I may be permitted to offer a few observations in reference to the true rank and importance of the subject with which Political Economy is conversant.

Any weight that may attach to the class of objections we are now considering is largely due to the form in which the advocates of the materialistic sciences too often state their case. The controversy

* Character &c., p. 9.

as to the proper rank of Political Economy, viewed with reference to its subject-matter, is, in truth, only one phase of the wider controversy of Plato *v.* Bacon, of which Lord Macaulay treats in his essay on the last-named philosopher. If we want a fair specimen of the class of arguments by which the advocates of the Baconian side sometimes attempt to support their case, we need only turn to the essay just mentioned.* It is a calumny on Lord Bacon to say that "the aim of his philosophy was to supply our vulgar wants." It is a fact that Lord Bacon set a high value upon physical comforts; but no thinker ever had a clearer perception of the intimate relations which exist between the physical, the moral, and the intellectual well-being of man. To say that wealth is a thing good in itself, and worthy to be pursued for its own sake, irrespective of the consequences to which its pursuit may lead, is one thing; to say that the subject "wealth" is a subject of the first importance as a link in a chain of causation, is another and a quite different thing. It is unfortunately true that Economists some-

---

* Take, for instance, the following passage: "The aim of the Platonic Philosophy was to raise us far above vulgar wants. The aim of the Baconian philosophy was to supply our vulgar wants. The former aim was noble, but the latter was attainable." Of this passage it has been pointedly said that, "on the contrary, the former aim was both noble, and to many men attainable, the latter not only ignoble, but to all men unattainable, and to the noblest most." (John Mitchel, in the Jail Journal.) The whole Essay furnishes a good example of how much may be done by a brilliant style and a richly-stored memory towards making a very little thought go a very long way.

3

times speak as though to produce the greatest possible amount of wealth with the least possible expenditure of labour were the one great object which the law-makers of every civilised nation ought to set before themselves, and to which every other consideration ought to be sacrificed. Speaking of England, Sismondi observes with much force : "In this astonishing country, which seems to be submitted to a great experiment for the instruction of the rest of the world, I have seen production increasing while enjoyments were diminishing. The mass of the nation there, no less than the philosophers, seem to forget that the increase of wealth is not the end in Political Economy, but its instrument in procuring the happiness of all. I sought for this happiness in every class and could nowhere find it."* It is, perhaps, not too much to say that in the chief wealth-producing centres of England the physical and moral degradation of human nature is greater both in extent and degree, the average of misery and hopeless wretchedness is higher than amongst any other populations of equal numbers on the face of the earth. "British industrial existence," writes Mr. Carlyle, "seems fast becoming one large poison swamp of reeking pestilence, physical and moral ; a hideous living Golgotha of souls and bodies buried alive, such a Curtius gulph communicating with the nether deeps as the sun never saw till now."†

* See the preface to the "New Principles of Political Economy."
† Latter-Day Pamphlets—*The Present Time.*

If I might presume to imitate the method of Berkeley, I would put to some dogmatic, self-satisfied British Economist, the following query as worthy of his consideration : " Whether it be not an obvious fact that the average of human happiness is far higher amongst the laziest populations of Spain or southern Italy than in the great industrial centres of England ?"

The line of thought rather suggested than followed out in the foregoing observations would probably lead us to question the doctrine that the largest production of wealth at the least cost of labour is the *summum bonum*. But, as already pointed out, we may consistently reject this doctrine *in toto*, and yet hold that " wealth," viewed as a cause and not as an ultimate aim, is a subject of the first importance. We must not be too quick to conclude that the relation between the large production of wealth in the districts we have been referring to, and the high average of human misery is necessarily and essentially a relation of cause and effect. Before arriving at any such conclusion, we should have to consider certain questions affecting the distribution as well as the nature and production of wealth,—questions the great importance of which few will deny, but as regards the true answers to which men have differed and do differ widely. The fact is that we cannot fully appreciate the importance of the subject " wealth" until we have realised the nature and magnitude of the effects which are plainly traceable to the presence or absence of

wealth as their cause. We may or we may not hold
that the great inequality in the distribution of wealth
which marks our social system is a necessary evil;
but we cannot shut our eyes to the terrible consequences of which that inequality is the cause. There
are certain essentials, certain reasonable comforts, as
distinguished from luxuries, the presence or absence
of which serves, in a great degree, to mark the distinction between the outward life of the civilised man
and that of the savage or the mere brute. The
physical and the spiritual elements being closely
bound up together in man, it needs no proof to show
that anything which degrades or lowers man in his
physical relations will also tend to degrade or lower
his mental life. Now, poverty, as rightly understood,
always implies the deprivation, more or less absolute,
of the reasonable comforts above referred to. And
what does this deprivation import? For the weaker
or less noble natures it too often means a listless,
hopeless, half-brutalised existence, aiming at nothing
higher than, as far as may be, to satisfy the more
urgent physical needs. For the man whose nature is
strong enough and high enough to revolt against such
a life, it means a perpetual and grinding toil to make
life tolerable for himself and those whom he loves—a
toil which taxes all his energies for this object alone,
and leaves him no time for recreation or for the
exercise and development of the higher faculties of
his nature. It may be, and doubtless in a certain

sense it is very proper to preach resignation to the poor. But it is not the less true that, so far at all events as this present life is concerned, extreme poverty is a real and terrible evil. An American Economist, Mr. Henry George, in his book entitled "Progress and Poverty," quotes a saying from the Ramayan in which the truth on this subject is admirably epitomised. "It is not without reason," says Mr. George, "that the wise crow in the Ramayana, the crow Bushanda, 'who has lived in every part of the universe, and knows all events from the beginnings of time,' declares that though contempt of worldly advantages is necessary to supreme felicity, yet the keenest pain possible is inflicted by extreme poverty."* Side by side with this saying of the old Hindoo seer we may not inaptly place the advice given us by a modern poet. It is, to a great extent, the same truth, though in a different form, which is seen and exquisitely expressed by Burns, when he tells his young friend to—

> " Gather gear by ev'ry wile
> That's justify'd by honour ;
> Not for to hide it in a hedge,
> Nor for a train attendant ;
> But for the glorious privilege
> Of being independent."†

---

* "Progress and Poverty," p. 320. I shall have occasion further on to refer more than once to this remarkable book. The page numbers refer to the American one dollar edition.

† See Epistle to a Young Friend, p. 70 of the Globe Edition.

Referring to the class of objections now under discussion, M. J. B. Say observes : " Que l'economie politique ne s' occupe que des intérêts de cette vie, c'est une chose évidente, avouée."* This is certainly true in one sense. It is no doubt true that Political Economy is only directly concerned with the things of this life. But the laws and the forces of which Political Economy treats do not the less certainly affect the moral nature of man, because their action may be ndirect, or because there may exist inter-mediate causes through which they operate.

The foregoing observations are, perhaps, hardly within the scope of the present inquiry ; but I thought it as well to say so much in regard to the objections of those who question the dignity and importance of the subject of which Political Economy treats. Such objections, for the most, originate in a misconception, and cease to have any weight so soon as the case in favour of Political Economy is put upon a sound basis.

We may now turn to the second and more numer-ous class of objectors. The majority of men are willing enough to admit the importance of the subject with which Political Economy deals. What they object to is the teaching. They refuse to admit that the doctrines of the Economists can be accepted as safe guides by the Practical Statesman.

What rational grounds, then, are there for this

"Cœurs Oomplet d'Economie Politique," 3rd edition, vol. 1, p. 48.

disbelief in the teachings of Political Economy? It is hardly to be supposed that even in the case of those who take the trouble to acquire a fair knowledge of the Current Economy, the distrust is, as a general rule, due to any conscious preference of the inductive historical to the *a priori* deductive method of inquiry. The student naturally begins by assuming that his teachers are right in their method, and, if he puzzles at all, it is over difficulties that are more or less apparent on the surface. These difficulties, if he have time and inclination to think them out, may ultimately lead him to question the soundness of the method pursued; but that is a subsequent stage. For the present we will confine ourselves to those more obvious objections which may be expected to suggest themselves to a man of average intelligence, who reads some of the standard English text-books on Political Economy and tries to understand what he reads.

Let us suppose the case of a student commencing the study of Political Economy. Our student, we may assume, is fully conscious of the magnitude of the evils which, in our present social system, are traceable to the uneven distribution of wealth and the wide prevalence of poverty. The new science promises to tell him the laws which govern the production, distribution, and consumption of wealth. If our student be at all of a sanguine disposition, the programme which Political Economy sets before itself may well cause him to indulge in dazzling dreams.

"Surely," he will say to himself, "this science will tell me why it is that the good things of the world are so unevenly and so unjustly divided amongst men; why it is that they who work hardest and produce most too often receive least. And, perhaps, it will even tell me that there is a remedy for all this, and show me grounds for looking forward to a more just distribution in the not distant future." No one having a fair knowledge of the Current Economy will need to be told that hopes such as are expressed in the foregoing soliloquy must lead to disappointment. Our student, let us assume, begins his studies by reading Mr. Mill's book. If he has any previous acquaintance with the writings and the character of his proposed teacher, he will have learned to admire the courage and the devotion to truth with which Mr. Mill puts forward his opinions, without stopping to think whether or not they are likely to please his readers. He will feel confident that if Political Economy has really discovered anything radically wrong in the constitution of our social sytem, to which the prevalence of poverty is due, Mr. Mill will not hesitate to point out the evil, and, so far as may be, the remedy. In one respect at least he will find his hopes fully realised when he comes to read the chapter (b. ii., ch. 1) in which Mr. Mill deals with the solutions proposed by the Communistic and Socialistic systems. One cannot too much admire the courage, truth, and fairness which are displayed in this chapter. They form certainly a refreshing contrast to the ignorant cant which one is so often obliged to listen to when either Communism or Socialism comes to be discussed. No doubt Mr. Mill arrives at the conclusion that for the present and for a considerable time to come the establishment of any social system, based on either Communistic or Socialistic principles, must be regarded as impracticable ; "that the Political Economist for a considerable time to come will be chiefly concerned with the conditions of existence and progress belonging to a society founded on private property and individual competition ; and that the object to be principally aimed at in the present stage of human improvement is not the subversion of the system of individual property, but the improvement of it, and the full participation of every member of the community in its benefits."* But I am not at present so much concerned to point out the conclusions arrived at by Mr. Mill in reference to the merits of the systems just referred to, as to call attention to the opinion which he expresses as to the degree in which our present social system is capable of improvement. The passage I refer to is a remarkable one, and I shall quote it in full :—" If, therefore," writes Mr. Mill, " the choice were to be made between Communism with all its chances, and the present state of society with all its sufferings and injustices ; if the institution of private property necessarily carried with it, as a consequence,

* Principles, &c. People's Edition, p. 133.

that the produce of labour should be apportioned as
we now see it, almost in an inverse ratio to the labour
—the largest portions to those who have never worked
at all, the next largest to those whose work is almost
nominal, and so on in a descending scale, the remuneration dwindling as the work grows harder and more
disagreeable, until the most fatiguing and exhausting
bodily labour cannot count with certainty on being
able to earn even the necessaries of life; if this or
Communism were the alternative, all the difficulties,
great or small, of Communism would be but as dust in
the balance. But, to make the comparison applicable,
we must compare Communism, at its best, with the
régime of individual property, not as it is, but as it
might be made."* The passage quoted would seem
to contain two things :—(1) an admission on the part
of the writer that the present distribution of wealth
works such grievous wrong that the evils pointed out
as likely to result from Communism (and they are very
grave) are mere trifles in comparison; and (2) the
implication, if not the expression, of a belief that our
present social system can be so far improved as to
render it doubtful whether, when so improved, it may
not be preferable to the Communistic system. It is
obvious that this implies a very vast change. A state
of things which, considered with reference to another
state of things, is immeasurably bad, cannot be made

---

* Principles, &c. People's Edition, p. 128.

relatively good without undergoing a very complete transformation.

Finding, in the passage just quoted, such a marked confirmation of his hopes, our student is naturally very anxious to learn how the great change is to be brought about. And here he meets with his first severe disappointment. As he goes along he will find it laid down that the distribution of wealth corresponds to the three great agencies in its production—land, labour, and capital. He will find an attempt made to lay down the laws which, in our present social system, determine how the aggregate wealth produced is to be divided between the three classes—land-owners, capitalists, and labourers. But when he has reached the end of the work, and has stopped to sum up the practical suggestions which Mr. Mill makes for improving the present state of things so as to secure a juster distribution, his hopes for the future of Humanity will take on a much more sober complexion. In effect, the only suggestions which Mill makes for bringing about a more just distribution of wealth are the following :—(1) certain alterations in the laws of inheritance and bequest, with the object of "fixing a limit to what anyone may acquire by the mere favour of others, without any exercise of his faculties, and requiring that if he desires any further accession of fortune he shall work for it" (b. ii., ch. ii., secs. 3, 4) ; (2), the future appropriation by the State, by means of taxation, of what is commonly known as the "unearned

increment" in the value of land (b. v. ch. ii. sec. 5);
(3) restraint on population amongst the labouring
classes (b. ii. ch. xi. and xiii.); and (4) the practical
extension of the principle of co-operation (b. iv. ch. vii.)
Of these four remedies, the last two are obviously the
only ones which could be expected to operate upon a
large scale. Mr. Mill, and those who think with him,
hold that it is vain to expect any material amendment
in the present state of things until a very decided
change shall take place in the habits of the working
classes in the direction of an increased prudential
restraint upon population. But that any such decided
change will take place they do not give us the least
ground for believing: indeed, they hardly seem to
believe it themselves. Their great apostle and teacher
upon this subject expressly tells us that he has very
little hope of any decided change for the better.* As
regards co-operation, it is sufficient for me to point
out that co-operation properly so called—that is, productive co-operation—has been known and practised
in France for some fifty, and in England for some
thirty years. That the practice has done some good
in individual cases I do not deny. But its effect upon
the aggregate of poverty in the two countries named,
upon the inequality in the distribution of wealth con-

* See the "Essay on Population," 7th edition, 1872, p. 403. The
reader must not infer that I agree that the change in question is a
necessary or desirable one, or that it would produce the results expected by the disciples of Malthus.

sidered as a whole, has been so slight as to be hardly perceptible. Under these circumstances the onus of proof is clearly upon those who assert that co-operation is likely in the future to produce results far exceeding anything it has yet achieved. Up to the present this onus has certainly not been discharged.

The disappointment of our imaginary student will be severe in proportion to the magnitude of the philanthropic hopes in which he has indulged at starting. After a time, however, we may expect that he will recover his spirits and will commune with himself somewhat as follows :—" Well, if I have not learned all I hoped to learn, I have at least learned a good deal that is useful. True, Political Economy has not revealed to me any golden secret by which poverty with its attendant evils may be made to cease, but it has at least suggested some remedies by which the present state of things may be rendered more tolerable. Moreover, it has pointed out for me with scientific precision the laws which, in a social system such as ours, govern the production and distribution of wealth, and the phenomena of exchange and trade. About these laws at least there can be no doubt, and the knowledge which I have acquired of these far more than repays me for the time and trouble spent in acquiring it."

Here again, I fear the student is destined to be disappointed. He next proceeds, let us suppose, to read the works of some other Political Economist of eminence—say Professor Cairnes, or Mr. Thornton. He

is startled to find several of Mr. Mill's leading propo-
positions boldly challenged. He turns back again to
the book with which he commenced, and proceeds to
examine critically statements which on the first reading
he accepted with implicit belief. True, even on this
first reading, he may have met with much that he
found it difficult to understand or assent to; but then
we may well believe that he would have thought it a
foolish presumption for a mere beginner like himself
to set up to criticise or correct statements stamped
with the authority of John Stuart Mill. Now, however, his confidence in Mr. Mill's infallibility having
received a rude shock, he approaches the book in the
spirit of Descartes, determined to accept nothing on
trust. The result of this process, I venture to predict,
will be to modify very much his estimate of the value
of what he has learned. He will find that, according
to the meaning put upon the terms employed, several
of the leading theorems will be either untrue, or the
most barren of truisms. Other doctrines he will find
to be mere abstractions—creatures of the economic
imagination,—having no practical bearing upon or
relation to the actual facts of society. So, again,
several propositions enunciated as fundamental and
of universal application will prove, on examination, to be generalisations of the most crude and hasty
kind,—obtained by looking only at one side of the
case, and by ignoring the plurality of causes in problems of great complexity. Having reached this

stage in his investigations, our student may take either of two courses. He may throw up the study in disgust, convinced that it has little to tell him which is worth knowing ; or he may proceed to inquire how or why it is that doctrines such as those over which he has been puzzling his brain can have ever come to be propounded as important truths of Political Economy by thinkers of the rank of Ricardo and Mill. If he take the latter course, he will be naturally led to inquire into the question of method. He will call to mind certain ludicrous speculations of old Greek Philosophers regarding questions of Natural Science.* From these he will infer that even the very greatest thinkers are liable to fall into the most obvious errors if their methods of investigation be radically mistaken. These considerations will naturally lead him to a study of the writings of the new school of Economists already referred to. But we need not further accompany our imaginary student in his perplexities. The illustration has now, I think, sufficiently served its purpose.

We have seen that while the student is still in the condition of implicit trust, and before he has passed into the critical stage, the objections and grounds of

---

* See, for example, some of the physical speculations of the Timæus. Allowing the fullest weight to all that Mr. Jowett has to say in defence of these speculations (The Dialogues of Plato, vol. iii., p. 587 *et seq.*), they still remain a striking example of the absurd errors into which even the very highest intellects may be betrayed by a misapplication of the *a priori* method.

doubt which most naturally suggest themselves to him fall under two heads. These are (1) objections arising from the gloomy outlook presented to us by the Current Economy, and the absence of any suggestions affording a reasonable hope that the glaring injustices of the present system may soon be remedied ; and (2) differences of opinion amongst the teachers upon the most fundamental questions. As to the first class of objections, it may be said by the advocates of the Current Economy, that if the student chooses to take exception on such grounds, the fault is with him not with Political Economy. The business of the Political Economist is to tell the truth even where the truth is disagreeable. If, in so doing, he disappoints the hopes of philanthropic students, that cannot be helped. The student may be disappointed, and may feel disconsolate over the sad prospect disclosed, but he has no valid cause of complaint against the science. This answer would be conclusive enough if the teachings of the Current Economy on the subjects of population and wages were sound, and if the Professors did not make claims on the part of their science which its conclusions in no way justify. As to the first qualification I shall have something to say further on. As to the second, I have already quoted a striking passage from Mr. Mill, which affords an example of the kind of hopes Political Economists not unfrequently hold out to their readers. Instances of a similar kind might be quoted from other authors.

Take, for example, the following. At the conclusion
of his Primer, Professor Jevons, repelling with some
warmth the assertion that Political Economy is a
"dismal science," observes :—"Strikes are dismal,
lock-outs are dismal, want of employment, bankruptcy,
dear bread, famine, are all dismal things. But is it
Political Economy which causes them ? Is not our
science more truly described as that beneficent one
which, if sufficiently studied, would banish such dismal
things by teaching us to use our powers wisely in
relieving the labours and misery of mankind." We
may readily enough admit that Political Economy has
not caused the "dismal things" enumerated by the
Professor. No one, so far as I know, ever said it did.
But it is quite another thing to say that the science,
"if sufficiently studied, would banish such dismal
things." I sincerely wish I could persuade myself
that a sufficient knowledge of the Current Economy
was all that was needed to banish the dismal things
enumerated by Professor Jevons, and the still more
dismal fact that they whose work is hardest and most
disagreeable receive the smallest share of the produce
of their toil. For the present, however, I am at a loss
to understand how such claims can be seriously made.
The Current Economy does *not* show us any rational
grounds for hoping that such things as strikes, want
of employment, dear bread, and famine will be
banished from the world in the near future. What it
does endeavour to prove is that so long as human

4

nature remains such as it is at present, even in its best forms, and so long as our present social system continues to exist, the "dismal things" may be expected to exist also.

So much for objections grounded on the dismal nature of the science. We have now to consider the class of doubts which are suggested by the differences of opinion amongst the recognised teachers. This subject seems sufficiently important to justify us in devoting to its discussion a separate chapter.

CHAPTER II.

Differences of Opinion amongst the Teachers.

Men differ widely in opinion, and, in general, do not in the least know.—CARLYLE :—*Latter-Day Pamphlets.*

To most minds the word Science conveys the idea of accurate and verifiable knowledge—knowledge which does not admit of any differences of opinion when once its grounds are clearly understood. " Science," says Mr. Lowe,* " means knowledge in its clearest and most absolute form." And in a recently pub-lished English Dictionary,† which has been highly spoken of, I find the word science defined as " acknow ledged truths and laws in any department of mind or matter digested and arranged into a system." If the first word of this definition is to be regarded as essen-tial, it is not easy to see how Political Economy can establish a claim to be called a science. It is true, no doubt, as pointed out by Mr. Mill in his Logic,‡ that there may be a science which is not an exact science. It is true that " it is no disparagement to the

* Now Lord Sherbrooke. See an article in the Nineteenth Century for October, 1878.

† Stormonth's English Dictionary, 6th edition, published 1881.

‡ System of Logic, b. vi. ch. iii.; and to the same effect see Mr. Herbert Spencer's Study of Sociology, 3rd edition, p. 39-45.

science of Human Nature that those of its general propositions which descend sufficiently into detail to serve as a foundation for predicting phenomena in the concrete are for the most part only approximately true."* All this we may safely admit; and if the objection to the scientific claims of Political Economy amounted to nothing more than that its "general propositions" of the class described in the passage quoted were only "approximately true," its right to be called a science could hardly be disputed. But what shall we say if we find that the opinions of the recognised teachers as to the truth or falsehood of several of the most fundamental general propositions in the so-called science are hopelessly at variance, and, in many cases directly contradictory? It is hard to see how a branch of knowledge which is still in this condition can lay claim to the name of a science.

In the preface to his edition of the "Wealth of Nations," M'Culloch observes, in reference to the class of objections founded on difference of opinion, that one might as well question the truth of Astronomy because eminent authorities have differed widely in different ages. It ought to be hardly necessary to answer this argument. If it could be shown that all Political Economists of recognised authority who had written on the subject within the last fifty years were practically at one as regards the fundamental truths of their science, there might not be much force in the

* System of Logic, 8th edition, p. 434.

objection that they all differed widely from the French Economists of the last century. The argument from analogy is proverbially dangerous. M'Culloch's analogy might have some force as an argument if it could be shown that there were still, when he wrote, astronomers of eminence who held that the Sun went round the Earth. But failing that, or something to a like effect, it seems to me that the analogy is somewhat beside the mark.

Sixty years ago Colonel Torrens wrote :—" With respect to Political Economy, the period of controversy is passing away, and that of unanimity rapidly approaching. Twenty years hence there will scarcely exist a doubt respecting any of its fundamental principles."* An eminent English Economist, recently deceased, after citing "this unlucky prophecy," comments on it thus : "So far from the period of controversy having passed, it seems hardly yet to have begun;—controversy, I mean, not merely respecting propositions of secondary importance or the practical application of scientific doctrines, . . . but controversy respecting fundamental propositions which lie at the root of its reasoning, and which were regarded as settled when Colonel Torrens wrote."† This testimony is especially strong coming from a man like Professor Cairnes, who may be described as one of the ablest as well as one of the latest advocates of the

---

* Essay on the Production of Wealth, Introduction, p. xiii.
† Character &c., by Professor Cairnes, p. 2.

"orthodox" Ricardoan method of treatment. So, again, in a work by an eminent German Economist, I find the following :—"Anyone who has read a goodly number of idealistic works treating of public economy cannot have failed to be struck by the enormous differences and even contradictions as to what theorisers have considered desirable and necessary. There is scarcely an important point which the highest authorities may not be cited for and against."*

Those who are familiar with economic literature will admit that, in the passages just quoted, the case against the Current Economy is not in the least overstated. It is possible, however, that, amongst those who are not familiar with economic literature, this book may find readers who would care to have some evidence of the extent to which the maxim " doctors differ" has been illustrated by the Professors of the Dismal Science. I shall, therefore, proceed to briefly examine the recent history and present position of economic teaching upon two or three questions of the first importance.

1. There can be no more important subject in Political Economy than that of the causes which determine the rate of wages. All the suggestions which the Current Economy has to make for bettering the position of the labouring classes depend for their value upon the soundness of its teachings upon the wages question. The problem being,—what are the

* Roscher's Political Economy vol. i., pp. 106, 107,

causes which determine the rate of wages?—the solution until recently offered by all the leading English Economists was to be found in the formula, "wages depend upon the proportion between capital and population" as qualified by certain explanations. In the first place, it is obvious that, in whichever of the various meanings that have been put upon it we are to take the term capital, the theorem "wages depend upon the proportion between capital and population" is by no means strictly true. It is only a part of the capital of a country that can in any sense be said to pay wages. So also it is only a part of the population who are recipients of wages. The theorem, therefore, requires to be modified. The modification is thus given by Mr. Mill:—"By population is here meant the number only of the labouring class, or rather of those who work for hire; and by capital, only circulating capital, and not even the whole of that, but the part which *is expended* in the direct purchase of labour."* So qualified, the theorem is undoubtedly true; but I cannot see that it amounts to anything more than the arithmetical truism that the average rate of wages is equal to the total amount of wealth actually expended in paying wages, divided by the number of those who

* Principles &c., People's Edition, p. 207. The italics are mine. It is worthy of note that Professor Fawcett expressly speaks of the entire circulating capital of a country as constituting its wages fund (Economic Position of the British Labourer, p. 120.)

receive wages. How this truism can be propounded as a statement of the economic causes which determine the rate of wages, I am at a loss to understand. It is right to say, however, that this objection is clearly seen and attempted to be met by subsequent advocates of the doctrine. Professor Cairnes, speaking of Mr. Mill's statement and explanation of the current law, says : "The statements are such as may not be disputed once their meaning is clearly understood. At the same time, it must be freely confessed that it contains no solution of the wages problem. . . . The solution will be found in connecting these factors with those principles of human nature and facts of the external world which form the premises of economic science."* The law was subsequently re-stated by Mr. Mill in the following terms :—" There is supposed to be at any given instant a sum of wealth which is unconditionally devoted to the payment of wages. This sum is not regarded as unalterable, for it is augmented by savings and increases with the progress of wealth ; but it is reckoned upon as at any given moment a predetermined amount. More than that amount it is assumed that the wages-receiving class cannot possibly divide among them ; that amount and no less they cannot but obtain. So that, the sum to be divided being fixed, the wages of each depend solely on the divisor—the number of participants."†

* Some Principles &c., p. 187.
† Fortnightly Review for May, 1869, p. 515.

Of the doctrine so enunciated Mr. Mill says that it is taught " in every systematic treatise on Political Economy, my own certainly included."

This, then, is the celebrated Wages Fund Theory stated in its least objectionable form. Twenty years ago the doctrine, in one shape or other, was accepted by every English Economist of eminence, and was propounded by them all as the economic law of wages. Since then Mr. Thornton has attacked the theory with considerable vigour. In his work on " Labour," after giving his reasons for " utterly denying [the reality of any such fund," Mr. Thornton proceeds to make some observations which go far to explain why it is that Political Economy has suffered so much from amateur criticism. " The reader," says Mr. Thornton, " will have a difficulty in believing that notions so inconsistent with common sense and with everyday experience can be recognised dogmas of Political Economy. But, indeed, there are no notions too wild to become recognised if, because promulgated by authority, they are accepted without examination."* Mr. Thornton succeeded in making at least one very distinguished convert to his views. In the article in the Fortnightly Review, for May, 1869, already referred to, Mr. Mill professed himself convinced by Mr. Thornton's reasoning, and surrendered the theory which up

---

* Thornton on Labour, 2nd Ed. p. 88. On the same subject see also " Refutation of the Wage Fund Theory of Modern Political Economy," by F. D. Longe.

to then had been stamped with his authority. In this, as in every other controversy in which he engaged, Mr. Mill displayed a noble devotion to truth and an entire absence of personal vanity which it is impossible not to admire. Mr. Mill's conversion, following close upon Mr. Thornton's attack, gave to the then current explanation of the wages problem a serious shock. It seemed likely that the wages fund doctrine would soon come to be regarded as an exploded fallacy when Professor Cairnes came to the rescue. His explanation and defence of the wage-fund theory[*] must be allowed to be a very able effort to set up the doctrine again. Amongst Economists of eminence who have written on the question since it became the subject of controversy, the balance of authority seems against the doctrine once so universally held. The theory was repudiated by the late Professor Cliffe Leslie, and is, indeed, in one place referred to by him as " now rejected by almost all English Economists."[†]   So also Professor Bonamy Price expressly condemns the theory (Chapters on Practical Economy, pp. 183-188). Professor Thorold Rogers does not, so far as I am aware, expressly either accept or reject the doctrine. In his Manual of Political Economy he gives the go-by to the wage-fund theory, and propounds a theory of his own upon the wages question

[*] See Some Principles &c., pp. 185-221.
[†] See an Article on Political Economy in the United States, in the Fortnightly Review for October, 1880,

which has, at all events, the merit of being to a great extent original. Professor Jevons emphatically disavows the doctrine as being either untrue or a mere barren truism, according as it is understood.

The balance of authority amongst American Economists would seem also to be against the doctrine. It is expressly disavowed by Professor Thompson in his "Social Science and National Economy." Mr. Henry George, in "Progress and Poverty," boldly challenges not only the wages fund theory but the entire doctrine that capital is the source from which wages come. The eminent German Economist Professor Roscher of the University of Leipzig also expresses his dissent from the wages fund doctrine.* On the other side, Professor Fawcett, in the last edition of his Manual of Political Economy, as well as in his Economic Position of the British Labourer, expounds the doctrine in the old orthodox form. Upon the whole, it may be affirmed that the question is still undecided, but that the balance of recent authority decidedly favours the conclusion that the law of wages which is stamped with the authority of Ricardo,† M'Culloch, Senior,

---

* Political Economy, b. iii., chap. 3, sec. 166. See also an Article by Henry Sedgwick, on the "Wages Fund Theory," in the Fortnightly Review for September, 1879, in which the views of other foreign economists are referred to.

† See the 5th chapter of Ricardo's Principles &c., in which the wages fund theory is in effect taught.

Mill (till 1869), and Fawcett is either an absurdity or a barren truism, according to the interpretation put upon it.

2. The doctrine that wages depend upon the ratio between capital and population, whether true or false, would not necessarily impart a dismal complexion to the Current Economy, if it were not supplemented by the famous theory known as the Malthusian law of population. Here again we have a general principle of the first importance, about which the authorities differ to such an extent that there seems not to be the least hope of their ever agreeing. The question—What is the doctrine taught by Malthus?—is itself by no means easy to answer. His late explanations in reply to some criticisms of Mr. Senior's would seem almost to narrow the doctrine down to this :—that in the absence of certain counteracting influences which always have been, and may always be expected to be in active operation, population *would* increase until stopped directly or indirectly by want of the means of subsistence.* If this be really all that Malthus meant to affirm, then it hardly seems to me that the doctrine is worth all the noise that has been made about it. But this is certainly not the meaning which one would naturally take from the Essay on Population; nor is it the construction which has generally been put upon that celebrated essay. Malthus starts with stating

* See Senior's Political Economy, 3rd ed., p. 45, &c.

certain propositions as to the nature of the checks
which have hitherto prevented human population from
increasing at anything like the rate which, physically
speaking, it might increase at. He then proceeds to
prove his propositions by a most elaborate examination
of the causes which in different nations and at different
times have operated to retard population. The posi-
tive and preventive checks by which he asserts that
population has been held at bay, do not seem in the
face of them to have any necessary or essential connection with want of the means subsistence. It is
when he attempts to connect the two, and to show
that the checks which he affirms to be the immediate
causes of the comparatively slow increase of population
are, in their turn, caused by a want or insufficiency of
the means of subsistence,—it is at this stage that his
theory becomes the subject of fierce controversy. I
must say I cannot understand how anyone can read
the Essay on Population and doubt that Malthus does
attempt to connect his alleged checks to population
with a want of the means of life, and does therefore
affirm that there has been and is an actual (not merely
a potential) pressure of population against the limits
of subsistence. The connection is constantly dwelt on
in the course of his historical inquiry, and in the
chapter in which he sums up the result of that inquiry,
he begins by observing,—"That the checks which
have been mentioned are the immediate cause of the
slow increase of population, and that these checks result

principally from an insufficiency of subsistence will be evident" &c. &c.*

Upon the whole, I think I am justified in saying that in the Essay on Population the following propositions are affirmed :—

1. That in all thickly peopled countries there has existed, and does exist an actual pressure of population against the limits of subsistence.

2. That this pressure of population is a thing to be lamented, and that to it are to be traced several of the most glaring evils of our social system, including amongst others the low rate of wages and the consequent prevalence of poverty amongst the labouring classes.

3. That this pressure of population being thus evil in its consequences, ought to be, so far as possible, prevented, and that theoretically it might to a great extent be prevented by an increased exercise of what Malthus terms " moral restraint."

The portion of the doctrine embodied in the last of these three propositions has been much relied on by Mr. Mill and others as showing that the theory cannot correctly be described as dismal. But Malthus him-

---

* Essay &c., b. ii., chap. 13, p. 252 :—Professor Cairnes maintains that Malthus' meaning must be perfectly clear to any " candid or intelligent reader." But as it seems to me, Professor Cairnes shirks the only real question that can arise upon the interpretation of the Essay when he affirms and re-affirms that what Malthus meant to assert was the existence of a " tendency " in human beings to multiply faster than subsistence (Character &c., Lecture 7).

self expressly states it as his opinion that the remedy by increased " moral restraint," while abstractly possible, is by no means likely to be realised to any great extent.* Therefore, despite all that has been said on the subject, the fact remains that the teachings of Malthus are emphatically dismal. This famous " law of population" has been the subject of prolonged and bitter controversy. It is no part of my intention at present to estimate the force of the arguments on either side. I merely desire to point out the extent to which the authorities have differed, and do differ. But before doing so, I may perhaps be permitted to depart so far from the regular course of my argument as to point out the consequences to which the theory, if true, would lead.

It is only fair to Malthus to say that the restraint which he advocates is simply an increased exercise of voluntary continence. The disgusting doctrines preached by the Member for Northampton and others are a subsequent development of this branch of " Philosophy." But while it would not be fair to charge Malthus with having preached any such doctrines as last referred to, it does seem to me that his theory, were it true, would necessarily lead to some such results. The most bitter enemies of the Christian religion admit that its success in the direction of promoting voluntary continence among the masses of the people has been greater than that of

* See Essay &c., p. 403.

any other religion or philosophy which the world has yet seen. Some of the great philosophies of antiquity succeeded in producing individual instances of very admirable self-restraint; but their effect in this direction upon the lives of the common crowd of men was practically nothing. Viewing the matter even from the standpoint of a non-believer in Christianity, there does not seem to be any rational ground for hoping that any form of philosophy ever will arise the power of which to impose a voluntary restraint upon passion amongst the masses of mankind will be at all as great as that of Christianity. Malthus himself, in effect, admits that this is so. If, then, it be true that, despite all that Christianity has been able to do in this direction, and despite all the other motives which have hitherto held in check the tendency of men to increase their numbers, the pressure of population on subsistence has been such as to be the immediate and necessary cause of all the vice and misery referred to by Malthus, it certainly seems difficult to escape the conclusion that, if this vice and misery are ever to cease, it will be necessary to find some other means of checking population than is afforded by any degree of voluntary restraint upon passion which ever has existed or is ever likely to exist among the masses of mankind. We thus see that the "Fruits of Philosophy" is in a certain sense the outcome of the Malthusian theory of population. Hitherto the spread of the doctrines advocated by Mr. Bradlaugh and his friends has been held in check by the disgust and abhorrence which those doctrines have excited,—a disgust and abhorrence caused by what, I presume, Mr. Bradlaugh would call folly and prejudice, but what I prefer to term decency and moral instinct. Human nature being such as it is, it is not difficult to foresee the consequences which would ensue if this barrier of disgust and instinctive abhorrence were once effectually broken down.

Such being the Malthusian law of population, and such the consequences to which it would lead, it remains to inquire what is the state of authority as regards the truth or falsehood of the law, among well-known writers upon Political Economy and Social Science. The theory was first propounded as far back as the year 1798—that is eighty-four years ago. It purports to be the solution of a problem which is one of the most important in the whole range of Social Science. Professor Cairnes speaks of the law of population as " quite fundamental in the Science of Political Economy." We might fairly expect that by this time the authorities would have been able to agree upon some solution of the population question. But what is the fact? There has hardly ever been a time since the Malthusian law was first published when the hope of an ultimate consensus of authority as to its truth or falsehood seemed less than at present. Twenty or thirty years ago the authorities, at least in England, were almost unanimous in favour of the Malthusian law. At present, the doctrine is far from being universally accepted. In England, amongst recent economic writers, the number of those who accept the doctrine is still much in excess of those who dissent. But amongst the dissentients there is at least one whose authority upon questions of Social Science is of the greatest weight. If Mr. Herbert Spencer cannot be said to reject *in toto* the Malthusian theory of population, he certainly does dissent from some of Malthus' most important conclusions. He holds, apparently, that there has been and is, in a certain sense, a pressure of population upon subsistence, but he does not hold that the pressure is an evil, or that it ought to be or can be put a stop to by any exercise of " moral restraint." On the contrary, he says :—" From the beginning the pressure of population has been the proximate cause of progress. It produced the original diffusion of the race. It compelled men to abandon predatory habits and take to agriculture. It led to the clearing of the Earth's surface. It forced men into the social state ; made social organisation inevitable ; and has developed the social sentiments. It has stimulated to progressive improvements in production, and to increased skill and intelligence." And Mr. Spencer further holds that there are forces at work (irrespective of any special exercise of voluntary restraint) which are constantly tending to bring about, and must ultimately succeed in bringing about in this respect as in others,

an equilibrium between man and his environment.*
This is something very different from the dismal
theory of Malthus and his followers.

Among Economists proper, I find that Professor
Thorold Rogers, in his Manual of Political Economy,
is rather guarded in his comments on the Malthusian
theory (chap. viii.). It seems clear, however, that he
holds that there is not at present, nor is there any
reason to apprehend that there will be in the near
future, an actual pressure of population upon subsistence.

In the United States the doctrine is repudiated by
several Economists of eminence. Professor Thompson,
in his "Social Science and National Economy," under-
takes to show (1) that the facts of history are against
the theory; and (2) that there are reasons why the
theory cannot be true as well as facts to show that it
is not. So, also, Mr. Henry George devotes a book
of " Progress and Poverty" to an examination and
disproof of the Malthusian doctrine. Like Professor
Thompson, he reasons against the doctrine both his-
torically and deductively. Here, then, we have another fundamental principle about which, after eighty
years of discussion, the authorities are still at variance.

3. But the wages fund theory and the Malthusian
law of population need to be further supplemented
before the prospect becomes thoroughly and hopelessly

* Principles of Biology, vol. ii., part vi., chap. xii.; and see, in particular, passage at head of page 501.

dismal. For, after all, it is not easy to see why there should necessarily be a pressure of population on subsistence provided each man is able and willing to work in a world where there is plenty of work for a population many times as numerous as that which it at present supports. The missing link is supplied or attempted to be supplied by what is commonly known as the Ricardoan theory of rent,* involving, as that theory does, the law known as "the law of diminishing production from land." This celebrated law is thus stated by Mr. Mill: "After a certain and a not very advanced stage in the progress of agriculture, it is the law of production from the land that in any given state of agricultural skill and knowledge, by increasing the labour the produce is not increased in an equal degree ; doubling the labour does not double the produce ; or to express the same thing in other words, every increase of produce is obtained by a more than proportional increase in the application of labour to the land." Of the law thus stated he immediately adds : "This general law of agricultural industry is the most important proposition in Political Economy. Were the law different, nearly all the phenomena of the production and distribution of wealth would be other than they are."† In the law thus enunciated as "the most important proposition in Politi-

---

* As regards the true authorship of the theory, see Essays &c., by Prof. Leslie, pp. 383, 384.

† Principles &c., b. i., chap. xii., sec. 2.

cal Economy," we have a striking example of the sort of abstractions in which the Ricardoan Economists largely deal. It is not alleged that, as a matter of fact and as things really are and have been in the world, every increase of produce is or has been obtained by a more than proportional increase in the application of labour to the land. Such an assertion would be too obviously at variance with the facts. Mr. Mill admits that the alleged tendency "may be, and sometimes is even during long periods held in check." The law as stated and qualified seems really to amount to nothing more than this,—that were it not for certain causes which have been, are, and may be expected to be in active operation, it *would* be the fact, that every increase of produce &c. &c. And even this most abstract of laws, be it noted, is only alleged. It may or may not be true. No attempt is made to prove it; and, indeed, it does not seem very easy to conceive how such a law could be proved. As observed above, this so-called law forms the basis of, and is included in the Ricardoan theory of rent. The proposition that rent arises from the difference of fertility in different kinds of land, would by itself be obviously a mere abstraction which no rational being could accept as a statement of the causes which actually determine rent in a country like England. It is supplemented by the doctrine of "successive doses of capital" to the same land, with a proportionably smaller return to each dose. Ricardo's theory of rent is propounded and

elaborated with a skill which is certainly admirable in
its way in the 2nd chapter of his work on Political
Economy and Taxation. The theory may be said to
be epitomised in the following sentence taken from
the chapter just mentioned :—"Rent invariably proceeds from the employment of an additional quantity
of labour with a proportionably less return." The following more detailed statement of the law is taken,
with some slight alterations, from Professor Cairnes'
Character and Logical method of Political Economy*:—
" Agricultural produce is raised at different costs,
owing to the different degrees of fertility of different
soils ; owing also to this, that even of that corn which
is raised on the same soil, the whole is not raised at
the same cost. Now, in order that that portion of the
general crop of the country which is raised at greatest
expense be raised at all—that is to say, in order to
induce the cultivation of inferior lands, and the forcing
of superior lands up to such a point as shall secure to
the community the quantity of food required for its
consumption,—the price of agriculturul produce must
rise at least sufficiently high to indemnify with the
usual profits the farmer for this,—the least productive
portion of his outlay. . . . If, then, the price of
agricultural produce be such as to cover with ordinary
profits the cost of that portion of the general crop
which is raised at greatest expense, it will be *more
than sufficient* to cover with ordinary profits the cost

* 2nd Edition, pp. 188-190.

of that portion which is raised at less expense. There
will therefore be on all that portion a surplus value
over and above what is sufficient to replace the capital
of the farmer with the usual profits. And this surplus
value is the precise phenomenon of rent which it is
the purpose of the theory to account for." This, then,
is the Ricardoan theory of rent as stated by one of
its ablest defenders. The theory has frequently been
referred to by eminent English Economists of the deductive school, as a brilliant discovery achieved by
their method of investigation. There is certainly some
difficulty in understanding in what sense the law can
be said to be really active as a cause in determining
the rent of land in such a country as England. But
waiving all objections of this class, we will confine
ourselves, in this as in the former instances, to the
question of conflict of authority. In this respect, I
think we will find that the Ricardoan law of rent
is no better off, if indeed it be not worse off, than
the Wages Fund Theory, and the Malthusian law
of Population. In England, the weight of authority from Ricardo's time down to the present has
been in favour of the theory. I shall, therefore, as in the case of the Malthusian law,
content myself with referring to some of the chief
authorities on the other side. I may mention, however, that in this case, as in the cases of the two other
laws I have been considering, Professor Cairnes is one
of the latest as well as one of the ablest exponents and

defenders of (what I may term) the orthodox doctrine.*
Among living English authorities, I find that Professor Bonamy Price, in the 12th chapter of his
Practical Economy, examines the causes of rent. In
the main he seems to dissent from the Ricardoan
theory. He admits that relative fertility has something to say to the causing of rent; but he holds that
it is only one of many causes, and often a comparatively insignificant cause. Professor Thorold Rogers
treats the question of rent, in the 12th chapter of his
"Manual of Political Economy." Speaking of the
Ricardoan Theory, he says: "The theory is quite
hypothetical, and has absolutely no historical foundation. . . . It does not give any real account of
the mode by which rents have arisen and have increased." His definition of rent is, "all that remains
in the price at which the produce of land is sold when
the cost of production is deducted." This definition
seems to indicate that Professor Rogers, like Professor
Price, accepts in the main the teaching of Adam Smith
upon the subject under discussion. Amongst American writers of eminence, the balance of authority seems
to be against the Ricardoan theory. Mr. Henry C.
Carey maintained that the theory was in direct contradiction to the facts of history.† If the doctrine of
Ricardo be sound, it would seem to follow that the
peopling of the earth must have proceeded from the

* See Character &c. Lecture 8.
† See "The Past, the Present, and the Future,' by Henry C. Carey.

more fertile to the less fertile lands. Mr. Carey maintains that the direct opposite has been the case. In
this, as in others of his teachings, Mr. Carey has been
followed by many distinguished Economists, not only
in America but also in Europe. Amongst living
American Economists, his most distinguished follower,
so far as I am aware, is Professor Thompson of the
University of Pennsylvania. In his work on " Social
Science and National Economy," Professor Thompson
devotes 36 sections (secs. 94-129) to an examination
and historical refutation of the Ricardoan theory of
rent. On the other hand, Mr. Henry George is of
opinion, that "as to the law of rent, there is no necessity for discussion. Authority here coincides with
common sense, and the accepted dictum of the Current Political Economy has the self-evident character
of a geometric axiom."* The sentences which follow
show that by the "accepted dictum," Mr. George
means Ricardo's law of rent. And in a note he says
of this law, that "it has the sanction of all economic
writers, who are really to be regarded as authorities."
Mr. George is here,—to use an Americanism,—"rather
rough" on his own countrymen.

Let us pause here for a moment. We have now considered three fundamental principles of the Current
Economy. It would be hardly too much to say that the
three laws we have been considering are the most important of all the laws enunciated by the Ricardoan Eco-

* Progress and Poverty, p. 150.

nomists. Taken together, these three laws—the law that the rate of wages depends upon the proportion between capital and population, the Malthusian law of popula. tion, and the Ricardoan theory of rent—may be said to constitute the foundation of all the teachings of the Current English Economy as regards the causes which determine the distribution of wealth in our present social system. These laws have been the subject of discussion for more than half a century. They deal with subjects about which it is of supreme importance that the truth should be known. One would say, that if the subjects of wages, population, and rent are sus- ceptible of scientific treatment at all, the truth with regard to them ought by this time to be determined with such a degree of definiteness and finality as to negative the possibility of rational controversy. Yet, what is the fact? We have briefly examined the state of recent and present authority, both in England and to some little extent in other countries, as bearing on the three great subjects just mentioned. As the result of our examination, we have found that so far is it from being the fact that "the period of controversy is passing away, and that of unanimity rapidly approach- ing," that, in truth, the "period of unanimity" never at any time seemed farther off than it seems to be at present. If we object to the fitness of the name given to Political Economy by Mr. Carlyle, it will be on grounds quite different from those upon which the objection is generally based. A branch of knowledge cannot fairly be named a " dismal science," if, in truth, it be no science at all ; and I fail to see how Political Economy can maintain its title to the name of a science so long as its teachers are unable to agree about its most fundamental principles.

The objection here taken, be it again observed, is in no way met by the arguments of Mr. Mill and Mr. Herbert Spencer referred to at the beginning of the chapter. I am not making it a ground for objection to Political Economy, that some of its leading propositions are " only approximately true." If the authorities were at one in admitting even the approximate truth of the leading propositions, I would have nothing to say. The point I make is that the authorities have not yet been able to come to an agreement as to whether or not the propositions are true in any sense.

It must not by any means be supposed that the three leading principles which I have selected are the only specimens to be found in the writings of the Ricardoan Economists of differences of opinion upon questions of the first importance. It would be easy to multiply instances. Take, for example, the theory of Demand and Supply as affecting values and prices. That people in general should have somewhat vague notions as to the meaning of Supply and Demand, and the manner in which values and prices are affected thereby, is nothing more than we might expect But that radical differences of opinion upon a question apparently so simple and elementary should exist between such authorities as Mr. Mill, Mr. Thornton, and Professor Cairnes, is somewhat disheartening to the student.*   So again take the question of Cost of Production as affecting values and prices.   One would think that if it be possible for Political Economists to agree about anything, they might fairly be expected to agree as to the meaning of Cost of Production.   An analysis of Cost of Production is given by Mr. Mill,† of which analysis Professor Cairnes remarks that, as far as he knows, it "has been acquiesced in, either expressly or impliedly, by Economists alike in this and other countries."‡   Of the analysis sanctioned by such a weight of authority, Professor Cairnes says :—"It seems to me that the conception of cost which it suggests is radically unsound, confounding things in their own nature distinct and even antithetical, and setting in an essentially false light the incidents of Production and Exchange."§ Again, after pointing out some "practical errors of a serious kind," which result from this misconception of cost, he asks : "Now, what is the explanation of this singular confusion of thought and perversion of facts?"‖   This is certainly pretty strong language as applied to the teaching of Mr. Mill by one of his most distinguished disciples.

---

* See Some Principles &c., by Professor Cairnes, chap. ii. sec. ii., and chap. iv., secs. i.-iii. It is worth noting that all these authorities differ from Adam Smith as to the meaning and effect of Supply and Demand.

† Principles &c. b. iii. c. 4.   § Some Principles &c. p. 50.

‡ Some Principles &c. p. 47.   ‖ *Id.* p. 58.

I need not here refer at length to the Free Trade controversy; I shall have occasion to say something upon that subject in a subsequent chapter. It is a well-known fact that upon the question of Free Trade the teachings of the English School of Economists are set at defiance by the leading statesmen in several of the most advanced countries, and further that their doctrines are controverted by more than one foreign Economist of eminence.

There is one other doctrine of the Current Economy to which I shall briefly refer before concluding this chapter.

The distribution of wealth, we are told, corresponds to the three instruments of its production—land, labour, and capital. The share which goes to land, or the owners of land, is called Rent, that which goes to labour is called Wages, and that which goes to capital is called Profit. Profit, we are told, consists of (1) interest on capital; (2) compensation for risk; and (3) wages of superintendence. To this doctrine of the distribution of wealth several objections at once suggest themselves. In the first place, if we assume Profit to be constituted as above stated, the distribution of wealth into Rent, Wages, and Profit is not what it professes to be. It professes to be a distribution corresponding to the three instruments of production, and Profit is the share that goes to capital. But in the next breath we are told that Profit consists partly of Wages and partly of another element which, whatever it may be, cannot in strictness be said to form part of the share which goes to capital as such. No doubt it is true that the capitalist does, as a general rule, receive wages of superintendence, besides interest on his capital; and it may be convenient for some purposes to have a word like Profit to represent the aggregate share which the capitalist does as a matter of fact generally receive. But, then, we must be careful to understand what we mean by Profit. In co-operative Societies the labourers, besides their wages, generally receive interest on capital. To speak of Profit (in the sense above explained) as being the share which goes to the capitalist as such, is precisely as correct as if we were to lump together the wages of the labourer and the interest on capital which he may receive as the member of a co-operative association, and call the whole a part of the share which goes to recompense labour. So again, we have laid down for us the law which determines the rate of Profit; and we have also another and apparently a quite distinct law laid down, which is said to regulate the rate of interest. This is trying to one's patience. When we are told (1) that the rate of Profit is determined by a certain law; (2) that Profit consists mainly of interest on capital; and (3) that the rate of interest on capital is regulated by another and a distinct law, we would certainly expect to have pointed out for us the nature of the connection between the two laws, and how far the operation of the law of Profit is modified by that of the law of interest. No such explanation is given. The two laws appear to be, and are treated as being quite independent, and we are left to reconcile them as best we may.*

Amongst other criticisms which this method of treating Profit has called forth, I find the following in Professor Roscher's book:—"While most English Political Economists have confounded the personal gain of the undertaker† with the interest on the capital used by him,—many German writers have called the "undertaker's earnings" or Profit a special and fourth branch of the national income, co-ordinate with rent, wages, and the interest on capital. Yet, the net income of every undertaker is either the fruit of his own land used for purposes of production and of his capital, in which case it is subject to the usual laws of developement of rent and interest, or it must be considered as wages paid for his labour."‡ So again, Mr. Henry George, in "Progress and Poverty," criticises very severely the treatment of Profit in the Current Economy.§

The two questions :—(1) Is Political Economy as at

* See Principles &c., by J. S. Mill, b. ii. chap. 15, and b. iii. c. 23.

† Undertaker (German. Unternehmer) is here used in a sense corresponding to the French "entrepreneur;" the need of a corresponding word in English is pointed out by Mr. Mill.

‡ Principles &c., b. iii. chap. 5, sec. 195.

§ See in particular, b. iii. c. 1.—In connection with this subject may also be noticed the unmeaning and perplexing distinction between the treatment of the element of Risk as it affects Profits and as it affects Wages. As to this, see Some Principles &c., by Professor Cairnes, p. 82, st seq., and an article by Prof. Leslie in the Fortnightly Review for November, 1881.

present taught entitled to be called a science? and (2) Is the subject-matter of Political Economy susceptible of scientific treatment?—are obviously distinct. In this chapter I have purposely abstained from attempting to answer the second of these questions. The two corresponding questions with regard to the existence or possibility of a science of society in general have each been the subject of a good deal of controversy. Mr. Lowe,* while he upholds the right of Political Economy to the title of a science, denies that there is yet any such thing as a Science of Society. "A science," says Mr. Lowe, "is not created by adducing arguments to show that it is possible." Quite so. But the observation has at least not as much force in the case of Political Economy as in that of the so-called science of Sociology. It may be that a science of the Nature, Production, and Distribution of Wealth can exist and will exist some time in the future. But until the teachers are able to arrive at something like agreement regarding the most important questions which they have to answer, the science can hardly be said to be yet in being.

* Now Lord Sherbrooke. See an article in the Nineteenth Century for October, 1878.

CHAPTER III.

The Meanings of Terms.

Hoc enim habent notiones illæ generales et communes, ut in omni-bus disputationibus ubique intercurrant; adeo ut, nisi accurate, et anxio cum judicio, bene jam ab initio distinguantur, universo disputa-tionum lumini caliginem miris modis offusuræ sint: et eo rem fere deducturæ ut desinant disputationes in pugnas verborum. Etenim æquivocationes, et malæ acceptiones verborum (præsertim hujus generis) sunt sophismata sophismatum.—BACON :—*De Augmentis Scientiarum.*

LORD SHERBROOKE doubts that a Science of Society is possible, and denies that such a science exists. He holds, however, that it is possible and useful to abstract the economic phenomena of society from the rest and treat scientifically the phenomena so abstracted; and further, he holds that this has in fact been done, and that a Science of Wealth exists. We have seen some reason to doubt the latter proposition. It must be admitted that there has been plenty of time and plenty of discussion to mature a Science of Wealth if a Science of Wealth is ever to be matured. If we assume for the present that the economic phenomena of society do admit of scientific treatment, it will be a question of some interest to ask how or why it has come to pass that the body of doctrine commonly known as Political Economy is still so far from having attained to that certainty and precision which ought to characterise a mature science.

6

To answer fully the question just propounded it would be necessary to discuss the soundness of the method of investigation by which the laws of the Current Economy have been arrived at. There can be no doubt but that the Ricardoan method of reasoning deductively from abstract premises is largely to blame for the endless differences of opinion to which these discussions have given rise. If from amongst the complex network of causes which determine the course of a particular social phenomenon, the economic inquirer will insist upon abstracting one particular cause or class of causes and reasoning as though he cause or causes so abstracted were the sole influence determining the result, then it is more than likely that the conclusions arrived at by this process will differ from those of some other inquirer who looks at the question from a different point of view. It is the old story of the shield;—both are right after their fashion, but each is only looking at one side of the question. Ricardo tells us that the cause of rent is the different fertility of different lands combined with the law of diminishing return to additional labour and capital expended upon the same land. Other authorities tell us that rent is the result of the monopoly of land; others that rent arises from the fact that owing to causes, irrespective of monopoly, the price of certain classes of agricultural produce is always so high as to leave a margin after replacing, with the ordinary rate of profit, the capital and paying the wages of the labour necessary for their production. The truth will probably be found to be that in a country like England the phenomenon of rent, as it actually exists, is the result of all these causes in joint operation and of many other causes besides.

But while we may admit that the want of unanimity, like the want of authority which results from it, is ultimately traceable to a vicious method of investigation, there is at least one source of confusion, irrespective of errors in the general system of inquiry, which very materially contributes to aggravate the evil we have been complaining of. The source of confusion I refer to is the want of accuracy and certainty in the use of terms. Mr. Senior, indeed, goes so far as to say that if Political Economy " had possessed a vocabulary of general terms as precisely defined as the mathematical," it would probably have followed that " there would be as little difference of opinion among Political Economists as among mathematicians."* This is said upon the assumption that Political Economy is a strictly deductive science. Without going so far as Mr. Senior, we may allow that vagueness and fluctuation in the meanings of terms has been a fertile source of confusion in the Current Economy.

It would no doubt be easy to make the mistake of requiring a too high degree of exactness in the defini-

* See latter portion of Appendix to Whately's Logic supplied by Mr. Senior.

tions of Economic terms. Political Economy has, in fact, as Professor Cairnes observes, " been developed through the instrumentality of popular language," and " popular language has not been framed to suit the convenience of economic speculation, but with quite other. views."* From which Professor Cairnes concludes that " the precision of meaning which is so conspicuous in the nomenclature of Chemistry is unattainable in Political Economy."† This is true to a certain extent. Such terms as Wealth, Value, Capital, &c., have in common acceptance a very vague meaning. Each of them is surrounded, as Professor Cairnes has it, with " a vague aroma of association sure to suggest in particular contexts ideas which have no proper connection with the purposes of scientific research."‡ In dealing with such terms the Economist often finds himself obliged to choose between two evils. He must either leave the term as he finds it, or he may assign to it a meaning which shall be at once definite and suitable to the objects of his inquiry. In the first case, the term is sure to be vague and uncertain in signification, and such meaning as it has may not be exactly the suitable one. In the second case, the economic thinker finds himself subject to all the inconveniences which arise from using the terms of common speech in a sense more or less different from that in which they commonly are used. In the

* Character &c., pp. 144-145.   † *Id*., p. 146.   ‡*Id*., p. 146.

earlier stages of economic inquiry there is a further difficulty in the way of comprehensive and accurate definition. In order to define the terms of a science satisfactorily, it is necessary first to know what are the meanings in which, regard being had to the objects of the inquiry, it is most convenient that the terms should be used. That is to say, it is necessary to classify in suitable groups the facts and objects which form the subject-matter of the inquiry. But correct classification, in social studies at all events, does not become possible until the inquiry has reached a tolerably advanced stage. Hence the necessity of commencing with rough provisional definitions to be developed and amended as the inquiry proceeds.

It has been often charged against Adam Smith that he has neglected to give definitions of his principal terms. On this Mr. Senior observes : " The great defect of Adam Smith and of our own Economists in general is the want of definitions." The charge has more force as against subsequent Economists than as against Adam Smith. It is true that the Wealth of Nations does not contain many definitions strictly so-called. But the meaning of the more important terms used by Adam Smith is generally made sufficiently clear from the context ; and in the matter of adhering strictly to the one meaning, he is far ahead of most of his successors. Moreover, it must be remembered in favour of Adam Smith (1) that he wrote while the study was still in its infancy, and (2) that he never claimed for his economic teaching the precision and accuracy of a deductive science.*

The case of the Ricardoan or deductive Economists is less defensible. The science had now reached "a point at which definitions became urgently needed."† Moreover, these Economists did distinctly claim for their study the character of a deductive science, and treated it as such. It is not very easy to see how there can be such a thing as a deductive science whose principal terms are not defined with something approaching to accuracy and precision. We have seen that Professor Cairnes is to some extent an apologist for the defective definition of the Current Economy. Yet even Professor Cairnes admits and advocates the necessity of "clearness and distinctness of definition whenever terms of importance are employed."‡ On the whole, we may perhaps conclude that the least we are entitled to ask from the Ricardoan Economists is (1) that they shall define their more important terms clearly and precisely—taking care "where the economic sense differs from the popular one to bring into as strong

---

* I observe that Mr. Lowe, in his speech at the dinner given to celebrate the centenary of the publication of the "Wealth of Nations," did claim for Adam Smith the credit of "having founded a deductive and demonstrative science of human actions and conduct." This is certainly more than Adam Smith ever claimed for himself.

† Character &c., by Professor Cairnes, p. 138.

‡ *Id.*, p. 147.

relief as possible the points of difference ;"* and (2) that in the use of the important terms so defined they shall adhere strictly to the one meaning. We may now proceed briefly to examine in how far these requirements—and more especially the latter of them —are complied with.

In the appendix to Whately's Logic, already referred to, Mr. Senior enumerates seven terms which he calls the principal terms of Political Economy. He then proceeds to point out the ambiguities and confusions arising from the loose way in which these terms are used. It does not appear when this appendix was written. But, judging from the point in English Economic Literature at which the examination stops, I would say that it must have been written some forty years ago. If the appendix were to be re-written now and brought down to the present time, the number of ambiguities and confusions would certainly not be diminished. The terms selected by Mr. Senior are— Value, Wealth, Labour, Capital, Rent, Wages, Profits. The only one of these terms which I purpose dwelling on at any length here is Capital. As to the remaining six, the reader who may be curious enough to pursue the subject for himself will find in Mr. Senior's appendix a list of the ambiguities which had occurred up to the time he wrote. As to the term Value, if the reader will consult the 4th chapter of Professor Jevons'

---

* Character &c., p. 147.

"Theory of Political Economy," the 1st chapter of
Professor Cairnes "Some Principles of Political Economy newly Expounded," and pages 33-43 of Professor Bonamy Price's "Chapters on Practical Economy," he will find that the position of the term as
regards definiteness and certainly of meaning has
certainly not changed for the better since Mr. Senior
wrote his Appendix.   Again, as regards the term
Wealth, the reader may consult the last-mentioned
work (pp. 8 and 9), where Professor Price mentions
the fact that an eminent American Economist is so
disgusted with the confusions which have arisen from
the ambiguous use of "Wealth," that he proposes to
treat the term as Professor Jevons would treat
"Value,"—i.e., to do away with it altogether.

"The term Capital," says Mr. Senior, "has been
so variously defined that it may be doubtful whether
it has any generally received meaning."* At the
commencement of his chapter on Capital, Mr. Mill
observes : "The function of capital in production it is
of the utmost importance clearly to understand, since
a number of the erroneous notions with which our
subject is infested originate in an imperfect and confused apprehension on this point." The confusion
which has existed in reference to capital is also
strongly dwelt on by the late Mr. Isaac Butt, for
sometime Professor of Political Economy in the University of Dublin.   After alluding to Mr. Senior's

* Senior, Pol. Econ., 3rd edition, p. 59.

proposal to substitute " Abstinence" for " Capital," Mr.
Butt says : " Anyone who has really considered all
the fallacies and the confusion which have followed
from propositions supposed to state truths or arguments of Political Economy by the use of this most
uncertain and deceitful word ' Capital,' must feel
that in this proposal Mr. Senior does a service to the
cause of science which has never been sufficiently
appreciated or indeed understood."* Again, Professor
Price speaks of the subject of Capital as " singularly
liable to mischievous confusion, not only in the outside
world, but also among economic writers."† It would
be easy to multiply quotations to a like effect.

From all this we may infer that for a long time past
the leading English writers on Political Economy have
been fully alive to the fact that the subject of Capital
is involved in much confusion, and have perceived
how desirable it is that the confusion should be cleared
away. This makes it all the more strange, and all
the more discouraging to the student to find that the
confusion still exists. In proof that it does still exist
I might rely upon those of the passages just cited
which are taken from recently published works. But
in this case, as in that of the differences of opinion, it
will, I think, be better not to rely entirely upon the
evidence of others. Assuming here, as in the former
instance, that amongst the readers of this book there

* " The Irish People and the Irish Land," p. 13.
† Chapters &c., p. 103.

may be some not well versed in economic literature, we shall now proceed to examine somewhat in detail the various explanations of the term Capital, which are to be found in the Current Economy.

The following are the principal definitions or quasi-definitions of Capital given by the leading English writers* :—

1. ADAM SMITH :—" That part of a man's stock which he expects to afford him a revenue is called his capital." He then proceeds to divide Capital into fixed and circulating. Each kind of Capital is sub-divided into four classes, each class consisting, with one exception, of material objects. Food, clothes, &c., in the hands of the consumer he does not regard as Capital. Money is included among the subdivisions of circulating Capital (Wealth of Nations, book ii., chap. i.).

2. RICARDO :—" Capital is that part of the wealth of a country which is employed in production and con-sists of food, clothing, tools, raw materials, machinery, &c., necessary to give effect to labour" (Principles &c., chap. v. on " Wages").

3. MALTHUS :—"That portion of the material posses-

* When I speak of " English Economists" in this book, I use the phrase to include all writers on Economy who are commonly regarded as belonging to the English school. I do not, of course, mean to say that Adam Smith, Professor Cairnes, or Professor Cliffe Leslie were Englishmen.

sions of a country which is destined to be employed with a view to profit."*

4. M'CULLOCH :—" That portion of the produce of industry existing in a country which may be made *directly* available either to the support of human existence or to the facilitating of production" (Principles &c., 2nd edition, p. 97).

5. SENIOR :—" An article of wealth, the result of human exertion employed in the production or distribution of wealth" (Political Economy, 3rd edition, p. 59).

6. JOHN S. MILL :—"What Capital does for production is to afford the shelter, protection, tools, and materials which the work requires, and to feed and otherwise maintain the labourers during the process. . . . . Whatever things are destined for this use— destined to supply productive labour with these various pre-requisites—are Capital." And, again, " 'The distinction between Capital and not-Capital does not lie in the kind of commodities but in the mind of the capitalist—in his will to employ them for one purpose rather than another ; and all property, however ill-adapted itself for the use of labourers, is a part of Capital so soon as it, or the value to be received from it, is set apart for productive re-investment. The sum of all the values so destined by their respective pos-

---

* I take this definition at second hand from Mr. Senior's Appendix, already referred to.

sessors composes the Capital of the country" (Principles &c., b. i., chap. iv. sec. 1).

7. CAIRNES:—Does not give any definition of Capital, so far as I am aware, but divides it into fixed Capital, raw material, and wages-fund. (Some Principles &c., part ii., chap. i., sec. 8.) It would seem from the discussion as to the wages-fund doctrine contained in this chapter that by "wages" he means *real* wages, and that by "wages-fund" he means "the amount of the annual production appropriated to the labouring population," or "the amount of wealth which goes to support hired labour" (p. 195).

8. FAWCETT :—"All that wealth, in whatever shape or form it may exist, which is set aside to assist future production" (Manual &c., 4th edition, p. 18).

9. JEVONS :—"The aggregate of those commodities which are required for sustaining labourers of any kind or class engaged in work" (Theory &c., p. 214).

10. THOROLD ROGERS:—"The Capital of a country consists in its food, its tools, or machines, its money, in so far as that money is an instrument of production and exchange ; all improvements in the natural powers of the soil which tend directly to increase produce from the soil ; and lastly, the acquired skill or power of labour itself" (Manual &c., p. 60).

11. BONAMY PRICE:—"Wealth used for the purpose of producing fresh wealth" (Chapters &c., p. 103).*

* The reader will observe that the above list of definitions, or explanations, is taken exclusively from English writers, and only from

The first thing that strikes one in reading these definitions is that they differ very materially. Things which are Capital according to some of them are not Capital according to others. Take up, for example, money. Capital, as understood in common usage, would certainly include money. According to Adam Smith's explanation, money might or might not be Capital according to circumstances. The definitions of Ricardo, Senior, and Professor Price seem to exclude money. M'Culloch's definition clearly excludes money; and Professor Jevons' definition does the same. The definitions given by Malthus, Mill, and Professor Fawcett make the question whether money is or is not Capital, depend upon the intentions of its owner with regard to it. Professor Rogers also holds that money may or may not be Capital according to circumstances. In two respects the authorities seem to be at one. They all hold, firstly, that Capital is wealth of some kind, and secondly, that it does not include all wealth; that the extension of the term Capital is narrower than that of wealth. It is when they attempt to fix the special notes or attributes by which the species Capital is marked off from the genus wealth, that they become confused and cease to agree. If we exclude the meanings given by Adam Smith and Professor Rogers, which differ materially from all the

writers of eminent authority. If I were to include Economists of other countries or English writers of lesser note the confusion would be considerably increased.

rest, we will find, I think, that in the definitions selected the term fluctuates between three meanings. These are (1) all wealth which actually *is* employed in maintaining or assisting productive labour ; (2) all wealth which is of such a nature as that it *may be* directly employed in maintaining or assisting productive labour ; and (3) all wealth which is saved* or set apart by its possessors for the purpose of being employed in maintaining or assisting productive labour. These three meanings will, during the rest of this discussion, be respectively referred to as the first, second, and third meanings of Capital. It is obvious that each one of these three meanings differs very materially from the other two in regard to the test by which it is proposed to mark off Capital from wealth in general. The first makes the test consist in the wealth being actually consumed in assisting the production of more wealth. This meaning is open to one serious objection. According to it wealth and Capital would stand in a relation to one another which forcibly reminds one of Solon's celebrated saying about man

---

* A good deal might be said about the various meanings in which the word " saved " is used by English Economists. Enlarging on the theorem that " Capital is the result of saving," Mr. Mill tells us that " to consume less than is produced is saving " (b. i., chap. v., sec. 4). In another place he says :—" Since all Capital is the result of saving, that is, of abstinence from present enjoyment for the sake of a future good," &c. (b. i., chap. ii., sec. 1.) The word " saved " is here used in the latter sense, that is in a sense implying the exercise of the sacrifice of abstinence.

and happiness. It would be impossible to tell whether a particular class of wealth was or was not Capital until we knew the end. The second meaning makes the test consist not in the being used, but in the capacity to be used in a particular way. According to the first meaning, a loaf of bread might or might not be Capital according as it was or was not eaten by a productive labourer. According to the second meaning, a loaf of bread would always be Capital. The third meaning makes the test consist neither in the being used nor in the capacity to be used in a certain way, but in the intention of the owner of the wealth with regard to it. According to this meaning, it matters not what may be the nature of the wealth or to what use in the event it may be put ; provided the owner of the wealth for the time being have destined it to be used, directly or indirectly, in helping to produce more wealth, it is Capital.

The first part of Ricardo's definition seems to indicate that he understands Capital in the first meaning, while the second part leaves it rather doubtful whether he wishes the term to be understood in the first or second sense. The definitions of Senior and Professor Price also seem to amount to the first meaning. M'Culloch and Professor Jevons are clearly, and Professor Cairnes seemingly for the second meaning. Mill and Professor Fawcett are clearly, and Malthus seemingly for the third. That there should be so much difference of opinion among the leading Economists of a particular school as regards the meaning of a most important term would in itself be sufficiently perplexing even if each of them adhered strictly to the meaning assigned to the term by his own definition. But this is by no means the case. Take, for example, the following specimens from the writings of three eminent Economists all still living. We have seen that Professor Fawcett's definition amounts clearly to the third meaning. But a few pages after the definition I find the following :—" If a man has so much wheat, it is wealth which may at any moment be employed as Capital, but this wheat is not made Capital by being hoarded. It becomes Capital *when it feeds the labourers.*"* This is the first meaning plainly enough. It is evident that if the wheat only becomes Capital when it feeds the labourers, it is not made Capital merely by being set aside to assist future production. Again, we have seen that the definition given by Professor Jevons, in his Theory of Political Economy, states the second meaning as the proper one for Capital. In his Primer, however, he tells us that Capital " consists of wealth used to help us in producing more wealth " (chap. v.), which seems to indicate that he here understands Capital in the first meaning; while again, in the Theory (p. 233), he treats money as a part of Capital which is inconsistent certainly with the second and seemingly with the first meaning. I have said that Professor Price's definition

* Manual &c., p. 30. The italics are mine.

seems to adopt the test suggested by the first meaning. Any doubts that might exist as to the meaning of the definition is removed by the subsequent explanations. Thus Professor Price is of opinion that the being " consumed and destroyed in the process of creating wealth" is the " necessary and universal test " of Capital or not-Capital (pp. 103, 104). But on the very next page he says : " As to land, it seems to me impossible not to accept it as Capital. It is undeniably pre-existing wealth necessary as an instrument of production; it thus falls under the definition of Capital." It is not very easy to understand in what sense land can be said to be " consumed and destroyed in the process of creating wealth." Indeed, it is sufficiently obvious that the notes by reference to which Professor Price determines that land is Capital are quite independent of the note which he has just been insisting on as " the necessary and universal test" of Capital or not-Capital. An article of wealth may be " pre-existing wealth necessary as an instrument of production," and yet not be " consumed and destroyed in the process of creating wealth." Again, two pages further on, Professor Price falls back on his original test. He says, " An article cannot be declared to be Capital or not-Capital until the purpose it is applied to is determined." And, by way of example, he instances sacks of flour which, he says, are not Capital unless and until they are used to maintain productive labourers ; whereas it is quite obvious that, tried by the test by reference to which Professor Price determines land to be Capital, sacks of flour would always and necessarily be Capital no matter whether they were consumed productively or not. Truly, as Professor Price himself remarks, this subject of Capital is "singularly liable to mischievous confusion, not only in the outside world but also among economic writers."

In pointing out the endless confusion which surrounds the use of the term Capital in the Current Economy, I make no claim to originality. On the contrary, I have been careful to point out that the confusion here complained of has frequently been commented on by economic writers. It is this very fact that gives force to the criticism. Here is a term of the very first importance. It is admitted that the ambiguous and uncertain use of this term has been for a long time back a fruitful source of confusion: writer after writer has dwelt upon the necessity of clearing up the subject. And yet when we consult the most recent authorities, we find that the confusion so far from being explained away is seemingly worse than ever.

It is one thing to find fault with the attempts which others have made to solve a certain problem ; another thing to point out the right solution. Anyone who has ever watched a game of chess played by two good players, with critics looking on, will have noticed how often it will happen that a looker-on will be able to detect a mistake made by a player very decidedly his superior at the game. I have endeavoured to show that the most recent attempts made to clear up and explain the term " Capital" are themselves vitiated by confusions and ambiguities similar to those which they purport to explain away. The reader must not therefore infer that I claim to be able myself to clear away the confusion. The explanation of Capital seems to be to Political Economy what the trisection of the angle is to Geometry. Many have tried, but up to the present none have succeeded. In the remarks which follow I shall not attempt to do what so many others, in every way better qualified for the task, have failed to do. I shall merely indicate the way in which, as it seems to me, the operation of defining such a term as Capital ought to be approached. Even so much I do not attempt without considerable misgiving lest I may merit the title bestowed by Pope upon those who " rush in where angels fear to tread."*

In attempting to define an economic term, there are two requisites which should be kept clearly in view.—(1) the meaning of the term should be useful ; it should be suitable to the objects which the inquiry has in view, and for the purpose of advancing which the term is needed ; and (2) the meaning should be reasonably clear and definite ; the notes or marks selected for the definition should be sufficient to mark off the

* " Essay on Criticism," part iii. The reluctance of the higher intelligences in this case might be presumed to arise from causes other than those contemplated by Pope.

particular object or class of objects from every other object or class of objects of a similar kind, but not more than sufficient. Thus, when we define a circle as a curve, every point in which is equally distant from a fixed point known as the centre, we select a particular note which is sufficient, and not more than sufficient, to distinguish a circle from an ellipse, a parabola, or any other kind of curve. If we were to add to the definition some others of the various qualities which belong to the circle as distinguished from other curves, we would be making the definition unnecessarily involved. The notes or marks embodied in the definition would then be more than sufficient for the purpose.

The first of these two requirements is concerned with classification, and is by much the more difficult to satisfactorily comply with. It has been already remarked that before we can frame a useful definition of a term, we must have a tolerably clear idea of the class of facts or objects, or of the abstract quality common to a class of objects, which we need the term to express. Having got this idea, the next thing will be to assign to the term a meaning which will make it suitable for the service for which it is required.

Apply this now to the case of capital. In investigating the subject of wealth, the first thing that strikes us is that for the production* of wealth two things

---

* I do not say for the existence of wealth ; since, according to the definitions usually given, land itself is wealth before any labour has been expended upon it.

are needed :—there must be an exercise of human
labour, and there must be materials for that labour to
work upon. Hence we say that the primary and essential requisites of production are land and labour.
But a little consideration suffices to show us that for
the production of wealth, as it goes on in the world of
to-day, there is a third requisite. Labour would not
be anything like as productive as it is were it not for
the division of employments, and the existence of
various articles of wealth which assist labour and render
it more efficient. But the division of labour could not
be carried to any great extent unless each labourer
was able to procure in exchange the necessaries of
existence, so as to dispense him from the obligation
of producing those necessaries for himself. We thus
get a general rough outline of the nature of the third
requisite to production in its more advanced forms.
At each moment of time there must exist in the community, or within the orbit of exchange, a certain
quantity of wealth available for the maintenance and
assistance of productive labour. It becomes advisable
to examine the nature and functions of this third requisite a little more in detail ; and before doing so, it
is well to select, or if need be, to coin a term by which
to represent it. In common speech the only term
which at all comes near to having the desired meaning
is Capital. The meaning of that term, however, in
common speech is vague in the extreme, and it will
require to be made a good deal more definite before

it can safely be used as a scientific term. Still it is a
term of common speech, and as Political Economy is
committed to the policy of taking its terms from common speech rather than coining new ones, we will
adopt Capital, and try to make it serve our purpose
as well as may be. Now, Capital is *ex hypothesi*
wealth of some kind. The question is, does it include
all wealth ? in which case there is hardly any need of
a new term. Or is it only a part of wealth ? And if the
latter, then what are the notes by which it is expedient
to mark off the particular class of objects constituting
the extension of Capital from the wider class constituting the extension of wealth. It is evident, in the first
place, that the articles of wealth which are immediately
available for the maintenance or assistance of labour
are themselves the result of previous labour. Moreover, we have already set apart a term to designate
that agent in production which consists simply of the
raw material of the earth. It would appear, therefore, that the first note by which Capital is distinguished from wealth in general is to be found in
the fact that Capital is the product of labour ; no part
of the class of wealth which is included in land
can form a part of Capital.* Can we, with advantage, further narrow the class of objects of
wealth which it is expedient to include in the mean-

* I say this although I am aware that some eminent Economists
have (strange to say) maintained that land is Capital, while still
recognising the division of productive agents into Land, Labour, and
Capital.

ing of the term? The answer which naturally suggests itself is that Capital should be confined to those articles of wealth which are in their nature capable of being directly used in supporting or assisting productive labour. Such articles are food, clothes, and labour-aiding machinery. We have seen that the second part of Ricardo's definition seems to suggest this meaning, and further that this test is expressly adopted by the definitions of M'Culloch and Professor Jevons. I must say, that after giving to the subject the best consideration in my power, it seems to me that of the various notes which have been suggested as marking off Capital from wealth in general, the one just referred to is the only one which does not lead to confusion. We have seen that several of the leading Economists would make the test consist in the being actually used in maintaining or assisting productive labour. If we except the case of fixed Capital, this test gives us little or no assistance in determining whether any particular portion of wealth is or is not Capital. According to the definitions which make actual use or consumption the test, it would be impossible to say whether a sack of flour or a loaf of bread was or was not Capital, unless it had reached the hands of the consumer, and was just about to be consumed. "It is always extremely difficult," says M'Culloch, "to say when any portion of wealth is or is not productively employed; and any definition of Capital which involves the determination of such a

point can serve only to embarrass and obscure a subject that is otherwise abundantly clear."*

It must be admitted, however, that the definition of
Capital which makes the distinguishing note consist in
the capacity to be directly used in supporting or assisting productive labour is not free from objection.
It differs very widely from the common meaning of
the term. It would not include money as Capital. As
between individuals, it would make that man have the
largest Capital who had in his possession the largest
quantity of those articles of wealth which are directly
available for maintaining or assisting labour. This,
it need hardly be said, is very different from what the
phrase is commonly understood to import. It was
probably some such objections or criticisms which
induced Mr. Mill and his followers to shift the distinction from the nature of the materials themselves to
the intention of the owner regarding them. It makes
no matter, say these Economists, what the temporary
form of the wealth may be ; provided the owner has
destined it to be used, directly or indirectly, in producing more wealth, it is Capital. Now, if we may
assume that the object is to frame a definition which
will enable us in all cases to tell whether particular
wealth is or is not Capital, it is certainly not very satisfactory to be told that the distinction must be sought
in the mind of the owner. Moreover, once you bring

---

* Principles &c., 2nd ed., p. 97.   As to the subject being " otherwise abundantly clear," opinions may differ.

questions of intention and exchange into the definition, the effort to connect the conception of Capital with material objects leads to endless confusion. Land now becomes Capital in a double sense. In the first place, it is wealth which may be, and generally is, destined by its owner to be directly used in producing more wealth ; and in the second place land, like other wealth, is exchangeable, and may therefore, like money, be indirectly used in producing more wealth. In fact, it is of the very essence of the definition of Capital, as given and explained by Mr. Mill, that every conceivable kind of wealth is potentially Capital. Yet Mr. Mill, and those who define Capital as he does, all continue to recognise the classification of the agents of production as Land, Labour, and Capital. Adam Smith's distinction between wealth in course of circulation and wealth which has reached the hands of the consumer is open to the same objections though in a lesser degree. Whether a particular article of wealth in a man's possession is to be consumed by him, or is to be exchanged for something else, is still a question of the intention of the owner. Mr. Henry George, in "Progress and Poverty," is very severe on Mr. Mill for "remitting the distinction to the mind of the capitalist" ; but it seems to me that Mr. George himself does much the same thing when he says that Capital consists of such articles of wealth as "are yet to be exchanged." It is not easy to see how the distinction between wealth in the course of exchange and wealth in the hands of the consumer could be applied in the case of such a country as England, so as to fix any definite relation between her Capital and her general wealth.   But, assuming even that the test is such as to enable us to mark off with reasonable precision Capital from wealth in general, it may yet be questioned whether the distinction is one likely to be of service in economic discussion.   Mr. Senior and Professor Jevons criticise adversely this doctrine of Adam Smith's, that wealth in the hands of the consumer should not be regarded as Capital.*   If a tailor has in his possession a stock of food upon which he proposes to support himself while engaged in making clothes, this stock of food is discharging the primary office of Capital.   It is rendering possible the division of labour.   I cannot see that any object of economic inquiry is served by denying to this food the title of Capital, because it chances to be in the hands of the consumer.

Keeping in view the office which Capital discharges in production, we found that the note which most naturally suggested itself as marking off Capital from wealth in general was the capacity of being directly used in maintaining or assisting productive labour. We have now briefly examined the other notes by

---

* See Senior's Political Economy, 3rd ed., p. 64, and Jevons' Theory, &c., p. 245, *et seq*.   I cannot understand why Professor Jevons should suppose that, in differing from Adam Smith on this point, he is "at variance with the opinions of almost all writers on this subject."

which eminent Economists have proposed to mark off
Capital, and we have found them all to be unsatisfac-
tory or confusing. The natural inference would be,
that if it be expedient to give to Capital any narrower
extension than that of all wealth other than land, the
most suitable definition would be that given by
M'Culloch and Professor Jevons. The objections to
this definition have been already referred to. It might
be objected with some force, that a term which included only those articles of wealth which are directly
available for assisting production would not be likely
to prove useful, and might prove misleading in economic investigations. This objection might, however,
be met by being careful to explain that the amount of
Capital, as so defined, which might for the time being
be in the possession of a country or an individual did
not, as things are in the world, constitute any measure
of the power of that country or individual to command
the third requisite of production. The circumstances
upon which the power to command Capital depends
might then be explained.

But, it will be said, it is expedient to keep the
meanings of economic terms as near to the usages of
common speech as the circumstances will admit of.
As regards this argument, it may be remarked that if
we are to keep the meaning of the term Capital near
to the usages of common speech, we must keep it in
a very fluctuating state. Capital in common speech
certainly has sometimes a meaning which would seem

to have been present to Adam Smith's mind when he defined it as that part of a man's stock which he expects to yield him revenue. But when people use such phrases as "the vast Capital of England," they usually mean by Capital something which it would be hard, indeed, to distinguish from wealth in general. Perhaps the definition, "all wealth other than land," would come as near to the common meaning as any we could frame.

The result of the foregoing discussion may be briefly summarised as follows. It is doubtful whether it be expedient to attempt any definition of Capital which will make the extension of the term less wide than "all wealth other than land." If it be considered expedient to further narrow the extension of the term, then certainly the only way in which this ever has been done, and probably the only way in which it can be done in anything like a satisfactory manner, is by defining Capital as "all wealth which is of such a nature as to be directly available for supporting or assisting productive labour."

In concluding these observations as to the meanings of economic terms, I would ask this question : If it be true that Political Economists of eminence have not yet been able to agree as to the proper meanings to be put upon terms of such paramount importance as Value and Capital, what shall we say of the claim of the Current Economy to be called a deductive Science ?

CHAPTER IV.

The Current Law of Wages.

Whether the way to make men industrious be not to let them taste the fruits of their industry? And whether the labouring ox should be muzzled?

Whether, in order to understand the true nature of wealth and commerce, it would not be right to consider a ship's crew cast upon a desert island and by degrees forming themselves to business and civil life, while industry begot credit and credit moved to industry?—BERKELEY :— *The Querist.*

IN the second chapter of this book reference was made to the Wages Fund controversy. The nature of the doctrine and the present state of the controversy in reference thereto were there briefly set forth. It was shown that even in England, where the doctrine was at one time universally taught, the balance of authority is at present against it. But several of those who reject the Wages Fund theory in its strict sense still seem to cling to the doctrine that the rate of wages is in some way determined by the ratio between capital and population. Among living English Economists, Professor Fawcett, as we have seen, continues to teach what I may term the orthodox* doctrine. He regards

---

* The adjective, "orthodox," is in this book applied to the doctrines taught by the Ricardoan Economists. What is meant by the Ricardoan Economists has been already explained.

it as one of the elementary principles of Political
Economy that the circulating capital of a country is
its wages fund, and propounds, as a species of economic
axiom, the proposition that the average rate of wages
is regulated by the proportion between capital and
population,* So again, in his Manual of Political
Economy,† he says that "it is obvious that wages in
the aggregate depend upon a ratio between capital and
population." We have seen that Professor Price is
amongst those who expressly repudiate the Wages
Fund doctrine in its strict sense.   Yet it would seem
that he still holds that the rate of wages is in the main
determined by the ratio between capital and population.‡   Professor Jevons seems to me to be the only
English Economist of eminence who has entirely
emancipated himself from the doctrine that the rate of
wages is in some way determined or caused by the
proportion between capital and population.   In his
Theory, he denounces and exposes the Wages
Fund doctrine, and in the   chapter of his Primer
on "Wages" and "Trades Unions," the orthodox
doctrine is nowhere taught.

I own I find considerable difficulty in attaching any
definite meaning to the proposition that the rate of
wages depends upon the ratio between capital and
population, if it be once conceded that there is no such

---

* Economic Position of the British Labourer, pp. 120, 121.
† Book ii., chap. iv.   ‡ See Chapters &c., p. 198-201.

thing as a Wages Fund. It seems to me that thinkers like Mr. Mill and Professor Cairnes, having once laid it down that wages depended upon the ratio between capital and population, felt themselves coerced to qualify and supplement this by the Wages Fund doctrine in some shape or other. They saw clearly enough that, unless so qualified, the proposition would not be strictly true ; and that even in so far as it would be true, it would be too vague and indefinite to be of any practical use. Yet the fact remains that, while the qualifying doctrine has been to a great extent given up, the original proposition in the main holds its ground, and may still be fairly termed the current law of wages.

In this state of things I propose to examine (1) the way in which the current law is generally proved, and the extent to which the supposed proof really bears out the law; and (2) in how far the law is true, when understood in the only sense in which it is intelligible as a law of cause.*

The theorem that wages depend on the ratio be·tween capital and population is commonly arrived at in this way. It is first stated that wages are drawn from capital, or that labourers are maintained from capital; and if by wages we understand real wages,

---

* In the following discussion the existence of a general rate of wages is assumed in favour of the current doctrines. As to this, see on the one side Prof. Cairnes' Some Principles &c., Pt. ii., sec. 3; and on the other, Prof. Leslie's Essays &c., p. 181, *et seq.*

these two propositions are practically nothing more than different ways of stating the same thing. It is thence inferred that since wages come from capital, the total amount of wealth expended in wages must depend upon the amount of capital in the country, and hence that the average rate of wages must be determined by the proportion between the capital of the country and the labouring population. This argument seems, on the face of it, tolerably conclusive; but, unfortunately, it is vitiated and rendered worthless by one of those ambiguities in the use of terms which, as we have seen, are so common in the Current Economy. It is, no doubt, possible to understand the terms, "maintained from" and "capital," in such a sense as it shall be strictly true "that labourers are maintained from Capital." But if its terms are so understood, the proposition, although true, will not by any means justify the inference that wages depend upon the ratio between capital and population. What most of the leading English Economists really do is this. When they desire to show how obvious it is that "labourers are maintained from capital," they understand the term "maintained from," in one sense. When they rely on the proposition as proving that wages depend upon the ratio between capital and population, they use the term "maintained from" in another and a quite different sense. I am not aware that any economic writer has ever pointed out the existence of this ambiguity, or explained the confusion to which it gives rise.*

In the Current Economy we are constantly being told that those who deny that wages are drawn from capital forget that "the people of a country are maintained and have their wants supplied, not by the produce of present labour but of past," and that labourers " consume what has been produced, not what is about to be produced."† It is quite true, as pointed out by Mr. George, that those who argue in this way thereby imply that they are here using the term capital in such a sense as to include all the necessaries of life existing in a country, whether or not those necessaries come within the meaning of capital, as they elsewhere define the term. But they are doing more than this ; they are using the term " maintained from " in a sense which, if it be the sense of common usage, is most certainly not the sense in which Political Economists use the term when they tell us that while most labourers are maintained from capital, a few maintain themselves from the product of their own labour.

As regards the ambiguous use of the term capital,

---

* Mr. Henry George, in "Progress and Poverty" (book i., chap. iii.) refers to and relies on a corresponding ambiguity in the use of the term Capital. The conclusions arrived at in this chapter are, to a great extent, anticipated by Mr. George. But the process of reasoning by which they are arrived at is so far different from his that I feel justified in stating my objections to the current doctrines in my own way.

† J. S. Mill, Principles &c., chap. v., sec. 1.

enough has been said in the last chapter. It is only necessary to add here that in the following examination of the current law of wages, I am willing, in favour of the received doctrines, to give to the term capital an extension wide enough to include every species of wealth which, according to any of the definitions enumerated in the last chapter, could be said to form a part of the capital of a country. As regards the ambiguous use of the class of terms of which "maintained from" and "drawn from" are the most common examples, it will be advisable to go somewhat into detail. Before we can satisfactorily examine the current law of wages, it is necessary to clear out of our path, once for all, arguments of the kind referred to at the beginning of the last paragraph.

The class of terms under consideration, besides the terms "maintained from" and "drawn from," will often include such words or phrases as "consume," "live on," "draw their wages from," and such like. When it is convenient to refer to these terms or phrases as a class, we will, for the sake of brevity, designate them by the formula "maintained from," &c.

The nature of the ambiguity charged will be best made clear from an example. A is possessed of certain commodities coming within the definition of capital (whatever that definition may be). B, needing the commodities in question for his own consumption, goes to A and offers him in exchange certain articles of wealth differing in kind from, but equal in exchange value to the commodities owned by A. The exchange is effected, and B becomes the owner of and consumes the commodities which he requires. Shall we say that B is " maintained from" the wealth which he actually and in the literal sense consumes, or shall we say that the true source of B's maintenance is the wealth which, by the process of exchange, has been converted into the form adapted to his immediate needs? Let us try to make this a little clearer. When we speak of a labourer " consuming " capital, or " being maintained from " capital, we may understand the terms in either of two senses. (1) We may take them in their literal sense as having regard strictly and exclusively to the wealth actually consumed, or from which the maintenance is immediately drawn; and (2) we may understand the terms in, so to speak, a more scientific sense, as importing the notion of exchange, and referring not necessarily to the wealth actually consumed, but to the source from which the maintenance may be ultimately found to come after the process of exchange has been traced to its commencement. To be " maintained from " capital, in the second sense would imply something more than the actual consumption of capital for the support of life. It would imply that there had been a corresponding diminution in the existing stock of wealth, and would therefore exclude the case of a labourer who contemporaneously with the consumption of his maintenance, produces and gives in exchange therefor as much wealth as he consumes. Understand the term "maintained from" in the first sense and the answer to the question, "are labourers maintained from capital?" will depend exclusively upon the nature of the wealth which they actually consume. Understand the term in the second sense, and we will have nothing to say to the nature of the various forms of . wealth which the wages may assume in the process of exchange. It will be necessary to trace this process of exchange up to its source, and if the result of doing so be to convince us that the labourer is really exchanging the product of his labour for the wealth he consumes, we will deny that he is being "maintained from" capital.

For the sake of brevity and to avoid repetition, we will call the first of the meanings above ascribed to the terms "maintained from" &c., the ordinary meaning, and the second the scientific meaning. The nature of the ambiguity charged is now, I trust, made clear to the reader. The proof that such an ambiguity exists in the Current Economy has to some extent been already given. It requires but little study of the Ricardoan Economists to see that they generally use the terms "maintained from" &c., in what I have called the scientific sense. They all, or nearly all, speak of labourers as being maintained from capital *until* the product of their labour becomes finished and available for exchange. This way of speaking

seems to imply that if, and in so far as, the labourer
gives finished, exchangeable wealth in return for his
wages as he receives them, he cannot be said to be
maintained from capital. Again, they all recognise
the distinction between a labourer living on capital
and living on the produce of his own labour; which
clearly implies that in so far as labourers maintained
themselves by exchanging the product of their own
labour for the necessaries of life, they would not, in the
view of the writers, be correctly spoken of as being
" maintained from " capital. I suppose it will hardly
be alleged that when Political Economists speak of a
labourer as "living on the produce of his own labour,"
they mean that the labourer must produce by his own
labour the identical articles which he actually consumes for his maintenance. In a social system where
the division of labour largely prevails, the phrase in
question can only mean what in the Current Economy
it clearly does mean, viz., that the labourer lives by
exchanging the product of his own industry for the
things he needs. I think, then, I am justified in concluding without further argument, that what I have
termed the scientific sense is the sense in which the
terms " maintained from " &c., are most commonly
used in the Current Economy. The strange thing is
that the terms in question should ever be used in the
ordinary sense. It is only when Economists are
tempted by what seems a ready and conclusive answer to all objections to their law of wages, that they

are betrayed into the ambiguity here charged in the use of the term "maintained from." We have seen that English Economists frequently speak as though to say that labourers are maintained from capital were really nothing more than to say that the food, &c., actually consumed by labourers while they work is the product of former labour. When Economists speak in this way they are plainly using the term "maintained from" in the ordinary sense. They are assuming that the labourer is maintained from capital simply because the food which actually and in the literal sense maintains him is pre-existing wealth used to assist in producing more wealth, and wholly irrespective of the question whether he does or does not give wealth in exchange for it. Passages to this effect have been already quoted from Mr. Mill's exposition of the theorem "Industry is limited by capital." As a further specimen of the same sort of reasoning, take the following from Professor Fawcett's Manual of Political Economy: "The ploughman who tills the soil from which in the following autumn the harvest will be gathered is fed with the wealth which his master has saved; or *in other words*, the master *pays his labourer wages from* the wealth which he has previously saved."* Now, the man who ploughs a field adds to that field a certain additional value, which additional value is exchangeable; and is, as a matter of fact, in some countries at all events, not uncommonly exchanged for the very purpose of paying the

* 4th ed., p. 15. The italics are mine.

ploughman. Yet Professor Fawcett tells us that because in this case the wealth which is actually used in paying the wages, or which is actually consumed by the ploughman, is not the identical wealth created by the labour remunerated, we are therefore to conclude at once that the master pays the labourer's wages from the wealth which he has previously saved, wholly irrespective of the question whether he does or does not, contemporaneously with the payment of the wages, receive value in exchange therefor. Here, therefore, it clearly appears that the phrase " pays from " is used in what I have termed the ordinary sense.

Assuming that the reader is satisfied that the ambiguity exists, we may now proceed to examine its effects. The theorem " labourers are maintained from capital " will have two meanings, and may or may not be true according as it is understood. If we understand the term " maintained from " in the ordinary sense, it will be impossible to deny that labourers are maintained from capital.* The theorem will then amount simply to an affirmation of the fact that the food, clothes, &c., consumed or used by productive labourers come from the stock of the necessaries of life existing in the country. This is true of productive as it is of non-productive consumers. It is a mere truism, and in so far as the wages question is concerned a useless truism. I do not mean to deny that

* The reader will please to bear in mind what has been said as to the sense in which the term capital is used in this chapter.

it may sometimes be useful in Political Economy to state or call attention to propositions which are truisms. The fact that in a society such as ours, labourers do not, as a rule, actually consume the product of their own labour, but take their food, &c., from the subsistence fund existing in the country, is a fact which it is useful to bear in mind as showing the necessity of such a subsistence fund in order to permit of the division of labour. But when our object is to ascertain the causes which determine the rate of wages, the proposition that labourers are maintained (in the ordinary sense) from the common subsistence fund becomes an absolutely barren truism which gives us no help. So understood, the proposition is quite consistent with holding that, reviewing production as a whole, labourers do, contemporaneously in the strictest sense with the consumption of their wages, add to the store of existing wealth as much as they take from it. That is to say, the proposition so understood is quite consistent with holding that, viewing production as a whole, the wages of the labourers are in effect created by their own labour. It is evident, therefore, that, so understood, the theorem "labourers are maintained from capital" does not in the least justify the inference that "wages depend upon the ratio between capital and population."

We have next to consider what is the effect of taking the term "maintained from" in the scientific sense. This examination need not cause us much trouble. It has been observed that most differences of opinion would disappear, if people would only take the trouble to make sure that they mean the same things by the same terms. So, in the present case, having once ascertained clearly and definitely what we mean by saying that labourers are maintained from capital, we will be able to see, without much difficulty, in how far the proposition is true.

In how far, then, is it true that the wages of labourers are, scientifically speaking, drawn from the capital of their employers? Precisely in so far as they consume the wealth of their employers without giving fresh wealth in exchange therefor. In so far as the hired labourer does, previously to or contemporaneously with the receipt of his wages, return to his employer an amount of exchangeable wealth equal in value to what he consumes, he is not being maintained from capital any more than the labourer who maintains himself by exchanging the product of his own labour for the things he needs. To apply this test in practice so as to say in how far labourers in general, or any class of labourers in particular, are maintained from capital will not be very easy. In some cases it will be clear that the wages come from the product of the labour. In other cases it will be equally clear that they come from the capital of the employer. The residue, constituting probably a majority of the whole, will consist of those cases which do not clearly come under the one head or the other, and in which it will be difficult to say, with certainty, from what source the wages come. For example: a working baker produces a certain number of loaves each day, and receives his wages at the end of the week. If, as is pretty sure to be the case, the amount of finished exchangeable wealth which he has added to the store of his employer during the week exceed in exchange value the amount of the wages he receives at the end of the week, we will at once conclude that this is clearly a case in which the wages came from the product of the labour. The same will probably be true, in the main, of a tailor, a shoemaker, a basketmaker, and various other kinds of labourers.

Again, there is a large class of products known in Political Economy as "extractive" products, in the case of which the production of freely exchangeable value is, in the strictest sense, continuous and contemporaneous with the exercise of the labour and the receipt of the wages. Thus, take the business of stock-raising or sheep-farming. The product there is the steer or the sheep, as the case may be. The labour to be remunerated is that of the herd or the caretaker whom the stock farmer may find it necessary to hire. There is a large difference in value between a yearling and a three-year-old steer. But it is obviously impossible to draw the line at any particular time in the interval, and say, " Now, and not before this steer is a finished and exchangeable article of wealth." The increase in exchangeable value is strictly a continuous process. The labourer whose labour is necessary for the preservation and increase of the herd is constantly rendering to his master exchangeable value in return for the wages he receives. His wages are drawn,* therefore, not from the capital of his employer, but from the product of his own labour. The same is true, though in a less marked degree, of agricultural operations. The case of the farmer is a favourite illustration with Economists when they desire to enforce the truth that labourers are maintained from capital. They tell us that the farmer has to wait till the harvest time to reap the result of the labour expended many months previously, and that, in the meantime, the wages of the farm labourers must come from the previously accumulated capital of the employer. Now, as a matter of fact, a field that has been ploughed and has had the crop put in, is an article of wealth which may be, and often is, exchanged by the farmer. The additional value which is added to the field by the ploughing and seeding is just as freely exchangeable as the field itself was previous to the ploughing. I don't know what may be the practice of the English farmer on this head : but I know that in the Western States of America it is not an uncommon thing for a farmer to pay the wages of his farm labourers by raising the money upon the crop according as it is put in. In this case, also, it is impossible to draw the line at any particular point so as to

---

* The reader will please to bear in mind the sense in which the term ' drawn from " is now being used.

say, "Now, and not before, the product is finished and exchangeable." Here, again, the rendering of exchangeable value is a continuous process which goes on contemporaneously with the exercise of the labour and the payment of the wages.

It will be observed that in the foregoing remarks I have constantly spoken of "exchangeable" value; and I have made the answer to the question—in how far is it true that labourers are maintained from capital?—depend upon the further question—in how far is it true that labourers do contemporaneously or practically contemporaneously with the receipt of their wages, return to their employers an amount of finished or freely exchangeable wealth equal in value to the wealth which they consume? In requiring that the wealth created by the labourers be finished or freely exchangeable when the wages are paid, my position differs somewhat from that taken up by Mr. George in "Progress and Poverty."* He argues that it makes no difference whether the product be finished or not; and that since labourers are always creating value as they work, and in the vast majority of cases value which exceeds that of the wages which they receive, they are in fact always "putting in as they take out," and, therefore, wages never can be truly said to be drawn from capital. For example, he says, "as the rendering of labour precedes the payment of wages, and as the rendering of labour in production implies

* See book i., chaps. iii. and iv.

the creation of value, the employer receives value
before he pays out value ; he but exchanges capital of
one form for capital of another form. For the creation of value does not depend upon the finishing of
the product, it takes place at any stage of the process
as the immediate result of the application of labour.
. . . In the case of the steamship as in the case of
the pick, it is not the last blow any more than the first
blow that creates the value of the finished product.
The creation of value is continuous—it immediately
results from the exertion of labour."*

All this I do not in the least deny. I have shown
that the theorem "labourers are maintained from
capital," may be wholly true or only partially true,
according to the sense in which its terms are understood. It is, no doubt, possible to understand the
term "maintained from" in such a sense as that the
theorem shall be wholly false. Mr. George obviously
understands the theorem, "labourers are maintained
from capital" in such a sense as to imply a denial
that labourers do, contemporaneously with the consumption of their maintenance, give in return therefor value of any kind, finished or unfinished, equal
to the value of what they consume. So understood,
the theorem is wholly false, or is false with such trifling
exceptions as may safely be left out of consideration.
To admit this in the fullest degree is quite consistent
with the line of argument I have been pursuing. I

* "Progress and Poverty," p. 57.

have been endeavouring to ascertain, as far as possible,
the sense or senses in which the theorem, " labourers
are maintained from capital," is understood by the
leading English Economists, with a view to seeing
clearly (1) in how far the theorem, so understood, is
true ; and (2) in how far, as so understood, it justifies
the inferences that have been drawn from it.   In the
course of the investigation, I have been led to observe
that Economists frequently speak of labourers as being
maintained from capital *until* the product of their
labour becomes finished and available for exchange.
From this and other sayings of the Economists, I have
inferred that they would not regard labourers as being
maintained from capital, if, and in so far as, the creation
of finished or freely exchangeable wealth was contemporaneous with the payment of the wages.   But it
could hardly be contended that the construction which
English Economists put upon their own terms is such
as to coerce them to admit that labourers are never
maintained from capital, because, in a certain sense,
the rendering of value is a continuous process ; although
a considerable time may, in some cases, elapse before
the product becomes finished, and freely exchangeable
without loss.   We cannot, I think, deny that in the
case of most manufactured articles, there is a clear
distinction, as regards exchangeability, between the
finished and the unfinished product.   The additional
value imparted to a piece of cloth by cutting it up for
a coat may be, in a certain sense, exchangeable, but

hardly in the same sense in which the coat, when finished, is exchangeable. The rendering of value by labour may, in all cases, and under all circumstances, be a continuous process, but hardly the rendering of freely exchangeable value. Possibly the distinction may have little or no bearing upon the question involved in the wages problem. But it is an intelligible distinction, and a distinction which certainly is taken in the Current Economy. Before we undertake to show that a certain proposition is false, it is only fair to those who propound it that we should first endeavour to see in what sense they use it, and what it is that they mean to assert.

We may here summarise the results thus far arrived at. We have seen (1) that the theorem, "labourers are maintained from capital," as understood in the Current Economy, is ambiguous—the term "maintained from" being used sometimes in one sense and sometimes in another ; (2) that understanding "maintained from" in one of the two senses, it is undoubtedly true that "labourers are maintained from capital," but that the theorem, so understood, is a mere truism and does not in the least justify the inference that wages depend upon the ratio between capital and population ; and (3) that, understanding "maintained from" in the other of the two senses, the theorem is only very partially true.

So far, I have not attempted any disproof of the current law of wages. I have contented myself with showing that the so-called proof commonly given of that law is not really any proof at all. So soon as we clearly understand what is meant by the proposition, "wages are drawn from capital," and in what sense that proposition is true, we see at once that the very most we can infer is that the ratio between capital and population is one cause which, under certain circumstances, and to a very limited extent, may affect the rate of wages. But can we even infer this much? Mr. George says not, and that mainly because labourers are constantly rendering value of some kind in return for their wages.

In the second chapter of this book* we have seen that the current law of wages, as explained by Mr. Mill in his work on Political Economy, really amounts to nothing more than the arithmetical truism that if you divide the total amount of wealth actually expended in paying wages by the number of those who receive wages, the quotient will give the average rate per head. It is, certainly, not easy to understand how the law, as so explained, can have ever come to be propounded by Mr. Mill as a law of causation. It is, in truth, a statement of what *is* the average rate of wages, not of what *causes* the average rate of wages. The fact is, the thing comes back to what was intimated at the beginning of this chapter. It is impossible to give to the theorem, "wages depend upon the ratio between capital and population," any

* See *supra,* p. 39-40.

intelligible meaning as a law of cause, unless it is so explained as to amount to the Wages Fund doctrine. " To speak of the ratio of an aggregate wages fund to the number of labourers as determining wages in each country surely implies that the sum expendible in wages at any given time is a fixed quantity."*

In developing the current law, one is forced to choose either of two evils. If we explain it so as to make it intelligible as a law of cause, it ceases to be true ; if we explain it so as to make it true, it ceases to be a law of causation. Keeping these two dangers in view, I shall endeavour to explain the current doctrine in a way which will be least open to objection. The doctrine so explained amounts to this. In any given country and at any given time there exists a certain determinate fund of capital available for the payment of wages on the one side, and on the other a certain number of labourers seeking employment. The proportion between this fund of capital and the number of labourers is the immediate cause which determines the rate of wages. The amount of the capital fund as compared with the number of labourers is in its turn determined by two causes, namely :—(1) the average productiveness of labour; and (2) the extent to which the practice of saving prevails in the country. These last, therefore, are the causes upon which the rate of wages ultimately depends.

* Essays &c., by Prof. Leslie, p. 182.

Now, in the first place, it is evident that, even assuming the certain determinate fund of capital to exist as a cause distinct from the productiveness of the labour by which it is produced, it can at most fix a limit beyond which wages cannot go. What wages may be within this limit the law does not tell us. Again the limit is obviously of a most elastic character. Capital being itself created by labour, it is *prima facie* capable of being increased indefinitely with the increase of population or the increase in the productive power of labour. In fact the limit is so elastic that it is hard to conceive how, practically speaking, it can operate as a limit at all. But, further than this, capital, we are told, is constantly being consumed and renewed. The capital existing in a country is constantly changing. It is never the same for two consecutive days, much less for two consecutive months. If we are to adopt any definition of capital which would make it consist principally of the necessaries of existence, then the amount of available capital in such a country as the United States would be enormously greater after harvest time than at the beginning of summer. Is it alleged that the rate of wages follows these fluctuations in the proportion between capital and population? But, it will be answered, Economists never meant to say that on each particular day, and from day to day, the rate of wages is determined by the proportion for the time being existing between capital and population. All that they mean to say is that, viewing production as a continuous act, and taking the average amount of capital existing in a country during a reasonable period of time as compared with the average number of labourers seeking employment, the proportion between the two will determine what during that period will be the average rate of wages. No Economist, it will be said, ever meant to assert anything so absurd as that the rate of wages rises and falls with the temporary fluctuations in the amount of the wages fund arising from the continuous consumption and reproduction of capital. But here again it seems to me that the upholders of the orthodox law find themselves upon the horns of a dilemma. All Economists admit, what is indeed sufficiently obvious, that viewing production as a continuous act, the true source of wages is the produce of the labour enumerated. Thus Professor Cairns says: "The price of the product is the fund from which the remuneration of capital and labour—viewing production as a continuous act—is derived."* The product of the labour is always and obviously the ultimate source from which both wages and profits come; and here we have the admission of a distinguished upholder of the Wages Fund Theory that when production is viewed as a continuous act, the ultimate source becomes in effect the immediate source. But we have seen that it is only by viewing

* Some Principles &c., 2nd ed., p. 223, and to a like effect, see the same book, pp. 51, 61, 62, & 173.

production as a continuous act that we can give to
the current law of wages the least semblance of truth.
Hence we again arrive at the conclusion which we
were already led to by another path. The current
law of wages ceases to be an intelligible law of
cause the moment it is explained in such a way as to
be true.

But, it may be urged, even assuming the conception
of a ratio between capital and population as an immediate cause of the rate of wages to be a mere economic figment which has no existence in fact, it is an
innocent and in many respects a useful figment. It
serves as a stepping-stone and enables us to reach
and to firmly grasp the true and ultimate cause of the
rate of wages—the average productiveness of labour
and the tendency to save. But is this so? Even
assuming it to be true that the rate of wages depends
ultimately upon the productiveness of labour and the
disposition to save, is the supposed immediate cause
really so very innocent and harmless? On the contrary, I affirm that it is not only an unreal figment,
but an essentially mischievous figment. To borrow a
phrase from Professor Thorold Rogers, I would say of
the current law of wages that it is perpetually quoted
and is perpetually mischievous. Political Economists
of the English school are constantly referring to this
law as showing the necessity of putting some additional
check upon population. They assume that the ratio
between capital and population constitutes a cause

distinct from and independent of the productiveness of the labour by which the capital is produced. They forget that *primâ facie* there is no reason why every increase of population should not bring with it as a natural attendant a proportional increase of capital.

Let us look at the matter from another and a quite different point of view. Is it true, as a matter of fact, that the different rates of wages in different countries are caused immediately by the ratio between capital and population ? Take, for example, on the one hand, England, and on the other, any one of the Western States of America, say the State of Colorado.* In the necessary absence of reliable statistics, it is not very easy to prove that the accumulation of capital in Colorado is less in proportion to the population than in England. But it seems to me that even such general knowledge bearing upon the question as we have precludes the possibility of reasonable doubt. The population of England is certainly many times as large as that of Colorado. But the enormous capital of England is so far in excess of what can find profitable investment at home, that, as we all know, it is obliged to overflow and go to seek investment in every quarter of the globe. I find from a recent publication of

* I select Colorado as being the State which I happen to know best; I have no doubt but that the comparison would give much the same results if any other of the Western States, or indeed any newly settled country having great natural advantages, were selected instead.

the Cobden Club that the total value of the foreign investments of British capital is estimated by competent
statisticians at from £1,500,000,000 to £2,000,000,000.
In fact, in any discussion of the wages question, it
seems to me that one is quite justified in assuming
not only that the proportion of accumulated capital to
population is greater in England than in new countries
like Colorado, where capital is exceptionally scarce,
but even (if that were necessary to our argument) that
the proportion in England is greater than in any other
country in the world.   The onus of proof in such a
case rests rather upon him who denies than upon him
who asserts.

If, then, it be really true that the proportion between
capital and population is the immediate cause which
determines the rate of wages, we should expect to find
that wages would be much higher in England than in
Colorado.   The contrary, as every one knows, is the
fact.   Whether we understand by "wages" real wages
or money wages, the rate is much higher in Colorado
than in England.   Again, is it the fact that the different rates of wages in different countries depend ultimately upon the average productive power of labour
and the disposition of the people to save?   I have
already admitted that the productive power of labour
must fix a limit beyond which the aggregate of wages
and profits could not conceivably rise.   But that the
actual rate of wages in any particular country is
affected by the two causes just mentioned in the way

alleged in the Current Economy I utterly deny. To constitute an exact comparison between the productiveness of labour in England and in Colorado would be impossible. But in this, as in the former case, a few general considerations may enable us to get an approximate idea of how the matter stands. The reasons for saying that the productive powers of labour are greater in Colorado are (1) relative natural advantages in the production of what are known to Political Economists as extractive products, and (2) the fact that the bulk of the wealth produced consists of food and raw material, the value of which relatively to manufactured articles of wealth is necessarily high and always on the increase. On the side of England the advantages consist in that minute division of employments and extensive use of machinery which so enormously increase the productive powers of labour, and which in their fullest development can exist only in a thickly peopled manufacturing country. Mr. George would contend that these advantages are far more than sufficient to turn the scale. According to him "wealth is always greatest when population is densest," and "the production of wealth to a given amount of labour increases as population increases."* Let us assume, however, that, taking into account the exchange value of the products, the productive power of labour in Colorado is as great as in England. We

* Progress and Poverty, book ii., chap. iv.

would then expect to find that the rate of wages in the two countries would vary as the disposition of the inhabitants to save and accumulate capital.

Now the English people, as compared with other European nations, are not a people very much given to saving, but as compared with the dwellers in the Western States of America, they are a nation of misers. The motto of the average American as compared with the average European is, "Spend what you make and earn more;" and if this be so even in the Eastern States, it is so in a much greater degree out West. Has any one of my readers ever stood at the depôt in Denver, where the trains come in from the mining towns in the mountains, and watched the miners coming in to "have a good time" spending their wages? It is not an uncommon thing to hear those who have had their "good time" asking their incoming friends to lend them their fare back, inasmuch as they have not "one red cent. left." These men are strangely forgetful of the fact that the rate of wages, other things being equal, must depend upon the disposition of the people to save and accumulate capital. But then to be sure, the truth is not very forcibly brought home to them so long as they are in receipt of three dollars a day.

To sum up the results of this part of the argument: according to the law propounded by the Ricardoan Economists, the rate of wages depends immediately upon the ratio between capital and population, and ultimately upon the average productiveness of labour combined with the disposition to save. In Colorado, the ratio between capital and population is smaller, the average productiveness of labour is certainly not greater, and the disposition to save is much less than in England ; yet the rate of wages in Colorado is much higher than in England. That is to say, the state of things which actually exists is the direct opposite to what would exist if the current law of wages were true.

But it will, perhaps, be said this argument proves too much. If it be the fact that labour is not more productive, but if anything less productive, in Colorado than in England, and if the tendency to save be less effective in the former country than in the latter, then what cause can there be which will account for the difference in the rates of wages ? I answer, a very simple cause. The labourers in Colorado get a much larger share of what they produce than the labourers in England. This fact is, in its turn, due to a variety of causes, but principally, I think, to two causes. These are :—(1) In new countries landlords, as such, take but a very small share of the wealth produced. The produce is divided almost entirely between the capitalist and the labourer: and (2) the standard of living amongst the labourers is high, and they will not consent to work for the wages for which they work in old countries. So long as there is fresh land to be taken up the labourers can and will keep up this high standard of living and insist upon high wages.

In referring to the last-mentioned cause of high wages, we have touched upon a matter which strikingly exemplifies the contradictions and confusions involved in the current doctrines upon the wages question. If we look from the Western States of America to the Eastern States, from the Eastern States to England, and from England to some of the leading nations on the continent of Europe, we see everywhere exemplified the law that, *ceteris paribus*, the greater the disposition of the labouring classes in any particular country to live frugally and "consume less than they produce,"* the lower will be the rate of wages. And, indeed, the deductive Economists do not deny this. They all, from Ricardo down, tell us that it is possible for the labourers, by raising their standard of living, to raise the rate of wages, irrespective altogether of any change in the proportion between capital and population. Yet they tell us that the less the disposition to save or live frugally amongst the bulk of the population the less, *ceteris paribus*, the fund from which wages are to come and the lower the rate of wages.

That the immediate cause of high or low wages is the standard of living amongst the labourers—the wages which they will consent to take and work ; that

* Which, according to Mr. Mill, is the definition of saving (Principles &c., book i., chap. v., sec. 4).

the tendency of free competition as the accumulation of capital proceeds, and as the power of commanding capital passes more and more into the hands of a few, is to force down wages to the minimum which suffices to supply the labourers with the necessaries of existence—these are truths obvious enough to anyone who cares to see them. They are in effect admitted by the deductive Economists. The entire teaching, however, of the English Economists upon the wages question is based upon the assumption that wages are to be fixed by free competition, and that the principle of *laissez faire* is to be applied strictly to the relation of master and servant. No doubt, in our present social system, wages are measured in the main by competition. If English Economists confined themselves strictly to investigating the way in which our present system does, as a matter of fact, operate—waiving all questions of the rightness or wrongness of the system as outside the limits of their province—we would have nothing to say except, it may be, to express regret that they did not take a wider view of the province of their science. But some at least of them do take a wider view, and undertake to decide the rights and wrongs of the competition system in a highly dogmatic fashion. Among eminent English Economists who have written upon the wages question, Mr. Thornton holds a foremost place. In the second chapter of his book on "Labour," Mr. Thornton considers "The Claims of Labour and its Rights." He maintains to the fullest extent the proposition that the just and right wages of the labourer are simply what he can obtain in a system based upon private property in land and capital, and perfect freedom of competition. Take, for example, the following passages which are selected as specimens of Mr. Thornton's teaching upon this phase of the wages question :—"Freedom of competition means no more than that everyone should be at liberty to do his best for himself, leaving all others at liberty to do their best for themselves. Of all the natural rights of man, there is not one more incontestable than this, nor with which interference would be more manifestly unrighteous. . . . The dues of labour have nothing to do with either its needs or its value, and the only true criterion of wages is the agreement between the employer and the employed. . . . Taking advantage of other people's necessities is indeed the very essence of commercial enterprise, and is and always has been practised by all traders great and small. . . . Surely, if there be one right more incontestable and more indefeasible than another it is this,* and if this right be conceded at all, it must be conceded in its integrity, in all circumstances and despite of all consequences."†

This is honest and outspoken, at all events. In a certain sense, too, the propositions are undeniably

---

* The context shows that the right here referred to is the right of " taking advantage of other people's necessities."

† See Thornton on Labour, book i., chap. ii.

true. There can be no doubt that, according to the
laws which at present prevail in England and other
countries, the capitalist has a legal right (subject of
late to some slight restrictions) to take advantage to
the utmost extent of the necessities of the labourer.
There can be no doubt but that, as between master
and servant, the rights created by the agreement of
the employer and the employed are, as a rule, the
only rights which the law knows of. But Mr. Thornton is by no means content with this admission. He
illustrates his meaning by an example which I wil-
lingly accept as a fair test. He puts the case of the
owners of a life-boat refusing to take the crew off a
stranded vessel unless a promise is made that half
the value of the cargo will be given as salvage. Of
this proceeding he observes :—" Odious as the conduct of such salvors would be, their right to act in
the manner described is not to be impugned. There
is no intelligible sense of the substantive 'right' in
which it can be said that they had not a right to put
their own price on services which they were equally at
liberty to render or to withhold, and which, at
any rate, no one had a right to exact from them."
I feel strongly inclined to put three notes of
exclamation after this passage. But I will restrain myself, and will merely say that I differ from
Mr. Thornton, and most emphatically. deny that
the sense in which he here understands "right"
is the only " intelligible sense" of the word. One

may be permitted, with Mr. Ruskin, to doubt if the right of every man to profit to the uttermost by the desperate need of his neighbour would be allowed by Him who told how the master of the vineyard paid the full wages to the labourers that were hired at the eleventh hour, saying, in answer to the murmurs of the others : " I will give also to this last even as unto thee."

As I have referred to Mr. Ruskin in this connection, I may mention that the doctrine we have just been considering has excited his anger to a very unwonted degree. In his " Munera Pulveris" I find the following :—" I have no terms of English, and can find none in Greek nor Latin, nor in any other strong language known to me, contemptuous enough to attach to the beastly idiotism of the modern theory that wages are to be measured by competition." The reader will, perhaps, be inclined to think that in the matter of finding strong language, Mr. Ruskin has done pretty well, regard being had to the difficulties in his way. But it must be admitted that Mr. Ruskin has some reason to be angry. It is certainly not easy to read Mr. Thornton's exposition of the doctrine that free competition is the absolute arbiter of right and wrong, so far as wages are concerned, and keep one's temper. The principle that every man should be left free to take advantage of the necessities of others, has worked out some curious results in recent times. Wretched creatures barely allowed time for insufficient meals and insufficient sleep, and toiling all the rest of the twenty-four hours; mothers of families at work all day, and leaving their children to shift for themselves; little children condemned to hard physical toil, when they should be at school or at play:—these are some of the results which we have seen brought about in England by the application of the great principle of British Political Economy.

Not long since I read a paragraph in an English newspaper,* which is a striking comment on the theory that free competition can do no wrong. A young girl, aged 21, was brought up at the Middlesex Sessions, charged with stealing six jackets. "The prisoner, who cried bitterly during the proceedings, pleaded guilty." It appeared that the prisoner was hired to do sewing work at four shillings a week. The judge asked did she get her food along with that. The employer said not. For these wages the girl had to work from nine in the morning till eight at night. She was given the jackets for delivery, and she disposed of them to get food. She stated that she had had nothing to eat for three days. The detective who arrested her said " he had made inquiries in the case, and found that up to this time she had borne a good character as an honest, hard-working woman. When he took the prisoner into custody, he found her in a most deplorable condition ; there was no furniture in the place except a small table and a few rags in a

* The Newcastle Chronicle for March 27th, 1882.

corner, which served as a bed." The judge, " while commiserating with the prisoner," sentenced her to six weeks' imprisonment. And so the law was vindicated, and " right" was done. We have got so accustomed to this sort of thing that we look on it as quite a satisfactory vindication of the law to send a poor famished creature to gaol because, when the opportunity of getting food offered itself, she failed to exhibit a heroism of self-denial equal to that which enabled Sir Philip Sidney on the field of Zutphen to push away the cup of cold water from his own parching lips, and hold it out to the dying soldier at his side. " Oh, but," says the disciple of Mr. Thornton, " there was no wrong done to this girl. She *agreed* to work eleven hours a day for the wages of four shillings a week, and her agreement determined her rights. If four shillings a week meant starvation, and if she could get no more by ' free competition,' then however ' honest and hard-working' she might be, her ' right' was simply to work eleven hours a day for other people, so long as she could use her needle, and starve." If anyone ventures to raise his voice against the shocking injustice of this system, he is denounced as a sickly sentimentalist and a socialist, and heaven knows what besides.

Other results of the principle of *laissez faire* which have given some trouble of late years are impossible rents, evictions, fierce agitation, murder, and so forth. In America the same great principle has been relied on by the capitalists as forbidding any interference with the influx of Chinese labour : an influx which, if allowed to go on unchecked, would inevitably result in forcing down the standard of living amongst American and European labourers to a level far lower than anything yet reached. Fortunately, however, the law-makers in England and America have, to some extent, disregarded the teachings of the Economists. Recent legislation in both countries has not entirely conformed to the principle of *laissez faire*, and has even presumed to seriously interfere with the sacred right of every man " to take advantage of other people's necessities."*

But we have wandered somewhat from our subject. The question which I proposed to discuss was whether the current law of wages contained a true statement of the causes which, in our present social system, determine the rate or rates of wages. I have been led on to offer some general remarks upon the different and deeper question as to whether the causes which really are operative in determining wages, work justice or injustice. We will now return to the proper subject of this chapter, and conclude our criticism of the so-called law of wages. If the reader still have any lingering disposition to believe that wages are, in some way or other, determined by a ratio between

---

* Since the above was written, I observe that the President of the United States,—in this representing the capitalists,—has vetoed the Chinese Exclusion Bill.

capital and population, he will do well to act upon the suggestion thrown out by Berkeley in the second of the queries quoted at the head of this chapter. Let the student imagine for himself the case of a primitive community carrying on the process of production and exchange upon the terms that the land be common property, but that each man shall own the produce of his own labour. Assuming the division of labour to have developed itself to some considerable extent, let the student examine carefully what are the causes which, in such a state of things, would determine how large a share each particular kind of producer would be able to appropriate of the aggregate wealth produced. For example, suppose the case of a maker of hats. Would the real wages of the hatter—the amount of the necessaries and luxuries of existence which he would be able to appropriate—be determined by the proportion between capital and population existing in such a community, or would it rather depend upon the productiveness of the hatter's labour; this productiveness itself being a function of two variables, namely (1) the number of hats produced; and (2) the exchange value which hats might have in such a community relatively to the necessaries and luxuries for which the maker of the hats might exchange them? Having got so far, the student may now introduce the complications caused by the appropriation of land by individuals, and by the accumulation in a comparatively few hands of the

capital the existence of which is necessary to permit
of the division of labour. Let him then examine and
make as clear as he can the causes which, when these
complications are introduced, determine how large a
proportion of the product of his toil the labourer must
yield up in order to obtain the use of the land and
capital which are necessary to him. I do not say that
the task will be by any means an easy one. I believe
that the more remote causes which determine the rate
or rates of wages in thickly peopled countries are very
complex and difficult to understand. But I think that
the student who approaches the question in the way I
have indicated will have little difficulty in seeing that,
whatever the really effective causes may be, the ratio
between capital and population is not amongst them.
Indeed the famous chapter in which Adam Smith examines the complex causes which in fact determine
the various rates of wages in various employments, in
itself very completely disposes of the ratio doctrine.
The strange thing is that thinkers like Ricardo, Senior,
and Mill, with this chapter constantly before them,
could ever have come to teach what I have called the
orthodox law of wages. They would hardly have
done so, I think, were it not for the confusion as to
the true meaning and force of the proposition, "labourers are maintained from capital," which I have
endeavoured to clear up. That confusion being once
removed, it is not very difficult to see that the theorem
" wages depend upon the ratio between capital and

population" is about as true and about as intelligible a law of cause as if one were to say that the average amount of meat consumed by the customers of a particular butcher was determined by the ratio between the amount of meat in the butcher's shop and the number of his customers.

CHAPTER V.

Free Trade and Protection.

Whether the great and general aim of the public should not be to employ the people?

Whether he who employs men in buildings and manufactures does not put life in the country, and whether the neighbourhood around him be not observed to thrive?

Whether, if there was a wall of brass a thousand cubits high round this kingdom, our natives might not, nevertheless, live cleanly and comfortably, till the land, and reap the fruits of it?—BERKELEY:—*The Querist.*

UPON the subject of Free Trade the leading Economists of the English school are practically at one. I say "practically," because even here there is some little shade of difference of opinion. In his work on Political Economy, Mr. Mill concedes that Protection may sometimes be a wise policy, when imposed temporarily in hope of naturalizing an industry in itself perfectly suitable to the circumstances of the country.* But this concession is carefully limited, and, even as limited, it is much deplored by subsequent English writers. Professor Thorold Rogers says of Mr. Mill's qualification that it "is perpetually quoted and is perpetually mischievous:" and Professor Bonamy Price appears to be of a like opinion.† But putting out of

* Principles &c., book v., chap. x., sec. 1.
† Chapters &c., p. 315.

account this slight deviation of Mr. Mill's from " orthodoxy," we may say that all the leaders of the Eng-
glish school are unqualified Free Traders. This is,
moreover, one of the few questions about which the
Economists and the Legislators entirely agree. In the
first chapter of this book allusion was made to the
tendency recently manifested by certain Conservative
statesmen to coquet with the form of Protection known
by the name of " Fair Trade." But, so far as the responsible leaders of the party are concerned, the tendency has been only to coquet. Fair Trade may
do very well to damage the other side and win an oc-
casional election; but the responsible chiefs of the
Tory party are too wide awake to definitely commit
themselves to any such policy. On the other side, the
Liberal leaders are uncompromising Free Traders.
Indeed it has become the fashion now on the Liberal
side to treat the question of Free Trade and Protection as one that has passed out of the region of
rational controversy. One very distinguished member
of the present Cabinet has gone so far as to state that
in his opinion anyone who has not yet made up his
mind in favour of Free Trade is, by the very fact,
convicted of having no mind to make up. This is
hard on Prince Bismarck and men of his stamp. It is
amusing, too, to observe the way in which recent
writers in England handle the question. Professor
Bonamy Price laments the stupidity and perversity
which render it necessary for him to re-argue the

question. " One is tempted," he says, " to feel something of that mortification which a mathematician
would experience if he were compelled to demon-
strate anew the principles of the multiplication table;
and, in concluding his proof, he mournfully observes
" the demonstration is complete, yet conspicuous as is
its truth, it is resisted nevertheless."* In a similar
strain Mr. Farrer begins his pamphlet on the Fair
Trade controversy. He tells us that when asked to
write something in defence of Free Trade, it seemed,
to him as though he had been asked "to prove Euclid
or give a reason for the rules of grammar." So, again, it
is the fashion among English economic writers to speak
of the Americans in a patronising tone of pity and com-
miseration as a benighted people who are obstinately
bent on ruining themselves by pursuing a policy
which is obviously perverse and wrong. When they
condescend to argue the question at all, it is generally
in a tone which amounts to saying : " Well, really, it is
a hard case that at this time of day we rational beings
should have to argue such a question with you fools."

I believe it was the late Mr. Walter Bagehot who
proposed to limit very materially the application of
the Current English Economy by admitting that the
postulates or axioms upon which its teachings are
grounded are true only of England in its present stage
of development. Some such limitation is much needed
in the application of the Free Trade doctrines. The

* Chapters &c., pp. 300 and 314.

intolerant dogmatism which, in the Free Trade controversy, so often takes the place of argument, illustrates in a very marked degree the tendency of Englishmen to assume that what is good for England must necessarily be good for every other country also.

What I propose to do in the present chapter is this :—(1) I shall state the most important of the positions which, in my opinion, are really established by the arguments of the Free Traders. In favour of these concessions, I shall not deem it necessary to give any reasons ; quite enough has been said and written upon that side of the question in these countries. (2) I shall state the more important questions involved in the Free Trade discussion which seem to me to be still "in the region of rational controversy" notwithstanding all that has been said to the contrary. (3) I shall state and examine the arguments by which the advocates of universal Free Trade support their case. Here, as in the case of the wages question, we shall, I think, find that the arguments, when carefully sifted, obviously fail to bear out the conclusions based upon them. In the course of this examination I shall probably be led to state some arguments strongly pointing to the conclusion that the answers commonly given to several of the questions which I treat as open to controversy are wide of the truth. (4) Lastly, I shall very briefly glance at certain phases of the historical evidence bearing upon the controversy.

Before I proceed to treat of the four heads of discussion just enumerated, there is one very important aspect of the question with regard to which a few words of explanation may be useful. The Free Trade controversy has two aspects—the one social, the other economic. The advantages of the diversity of industry, the part which that diversity plays in the development of a people, these are questions in social philosophy much too important and too far-reaching to be fully discussed here. Assume it to be true that the aggregate production of wealth in the United States would have been greater had a much larger proportion than at present of the labour and capital of the country been turned to the production of food and raw material by a policy of Free Trade, does it necessarily follow that Protection was a mistake? If we are to say that the "greatest production of wealth with the least amount of labour" is the one thing to be aimed at by those who guide the destinies of a nation, the question just put is easily answered. It cannot, however, be denied that the growth of manufactures, the consequent rise of towns and cities, and generally the diversity of employments and habits of life, exercise a most powerful influence upon the social and intellectual development of a people. "Men's employments and daily industries react powerfully upon general character; variety of work produces and cherishes individuality."* Those who think with the present writer

* Professor Thompson in Social Science &c., p. 232.

that the class of considerations just referred to are proper to be taken into account by the practical states-man, will not be too quick to declare themselves for universal Free Trade, even if satisfied that universal Free Trade must tend to increase the aggregate pro-duction of wealth. English writers, as a rule, treat the question from a strictly economic point of view. This they have a right to do if they choose; but they ought to be careful to remember that they are looking at only one side of the question, and to limit their con-clusions accordingly. In the present chapter, I shall meet the English Free Traders upon their own ground, and treat the subject exclusively from an economic point of view. But I desire at starting to guard myself against being supposed to admit that Protection is necessarily condemned if, and in so far as, it can be shown that Free Trade leads to the greatest aggregate production of wealth at the least cost of labour.

We may now return to the point at which we digressed for the purpose of making the foregoing explanation. I proceed to consider in succession the four heads above specified.

1. The following positions appear to me to be estab-lished by the arguments of the Free Traders :—(1) That in the case of every nation which has passed a certain stage in its industrial development, a policy of absolute Free Trade is from an economic point of view the wisest policy. (2) That England has clearly passed the stage of industrial development referred to in the

last proposition, and had passed it when she first embraced a policy of Free Trade. (3) That for England Free Trade is not only an economically sound policy but is, under all the circumstances, the only practicable policy.

As already intimated, I do not consider it necessary to reiterate here the arguments by which the Fair Trade proposals have been met. Mr. Farrer's pamphlet is a sufficiently complete answer to the Fair Traders. But in his anxiety to show in the strongest light the advantages which England reaps from Free Trade, Mr. Farrer, so to speak, "lets the cat out of the bag." It appears from the first page, and from various passages of his pamphlet, that Mr. Farrer is a thorough believer in universal Free Trade. Mr. Farrer's facts and figures certainly show that England gains vastly by Free Trade, but unfortunately they show something more. They show that, in several respects, she gains *at the expense and to the detriment of other nations.* But of this I shall have more to say hereafter.

I may be asked to define what I mean when I speak of a certain stage in the industrial development of a nation. I admit it is difficult to draw a definite line in this respect. I doubt if it would be possible to explain the phrase in a way that would be at once definite and suited to the case of every country. Nor does this really constitute any objection to the form of my proposition. The particular circumstances of each country must be taken into consideration. The omission to do this, and the persistent treatment of Political Economy as a science which "belongs to no nation and is of no country" has been one of the chief faults of the Current Economy. When a country has become an exporter of manufactured goods to such an extent that its exports of this class of wealth far exceed its imports of a like kind, then we may say that this country has clearly passed the stage at which Free Trade becomes an economically sound policy. On the other hand, if a country have but a very small percentage of its population engaged in manufactures, if it be obliged to import nearly all the manufactured goods it needs, and to pay for the goods so imported entirely or almost entirely by the export of food and raw material, then I would say that such a country had certainly not reached the stage at which Free Trade becomes an economically sound policy. The turning-point would be somewhere between these two extremes. Perhaps we might say, with approximate general accuracy, that the stage of industrial development in question is reached when a considerable percentage of the population of a country is engaged in manufacturing industries which are of a kind suited to the country and which are firmly established and able to hold their own in open market. I may add that when I speak of "industries of a kind suited to the country" I mean either industries with respect to which the country in question has natural advantages, or industries with respect to which the country has acquired advantages, and is not, as regards natural fitness, in a position of marked inferiority as compared with other countries.*

There is one other observation which it may be well to make before proceeding to the second head of our discussion. The fact of England's having prospered exceedingly with Free Trade is not necessarily an argument in favour of universal Free Trade. It simply shows that England, when she took off her tariffs, had passed the stage at which Free Trade becomes the sound policy. It shows that Free Trade is good for England, not necessarily that it is good for other countries very differently circumstanced.

2. The following are some of the principal questions arising out of or bearing upon the Free Trade controversy which seem to me to be still undecided, notwithstanding all that has been said to the contrary. (1) Whether the exclusive, or all but exclusive devotion of labour and capital to the production of food and raw material, which in a newly-settled country with abundance of land naturally results from a policy

---

* As regards this last qualification it should, however, be remembered that, as pointed out by Ricardo and his followers, a country may, with perfect Free Trade, continue to manufacture a certain class of goods and export the same to another country having decided natural advantages with regard to the production of that particular class of goods, provided the last-mentioned country have still greater advantages with regard to the production of some other class of goods. The illustrations by which this is shown are familiar to every student of Political Economy.

of Free Trade, be, even from an economic point of view, a desirable result? (2) Whether it be a wise policy for any country to let itself become a mere draw-farm of food and raw material for other countries? (3) Whether history does not show that, even in the case of two old and thickly settled countries, having about equal natural advantages, it may happen that country No. 1 may, owing to special circumstances, so far get the start of country No. 2 in the race of industrial development as to make it practically certain that, so long as Free Trade between the two countries subsists, No. 2 can never hope to be anything better than a draw-farm for No. 1; and whether, when such a state of things has come about, Free Trade be an economically sound policy for country No. 2?

I say I regard these questions as still in the region of rational controversy. If it were not for the respect I entertain for certain eminent writers, I should be inclined to say that in the cases put by these questions, the balance of argument is as clearly against Free Trade as, in the case of England, it is in favour of Free Trade. For the present, however, my object shall be rather to show that in such cases as those just put, the gain from Free Trade is by no means so clear as the English Economists would have us believe. With this view, we will now proceed to examine the arguments by which the advantages of universal Free Trade are commonly supposed to be proved.

3. The case in favour of universal Free Trade is com-

monly rested by the leading English Economists mainly upon two great principles. These are (1) that in every country it is the wisest policy to leave capital and labour free to employ themselves in that branch of production in which the country has the greatest advantages, natural or acquired ; and (2) that all trade between two countries is really an exchange of commodities ; that, in the long run, the exports of a country must always balance its imports ; or, as the proposition is often tersely put, that " commodities are paid for in commodities."

The application of these two leading principles is somewhat as follows. In a natural state, or a state of perfect freedom, the motives which actuate men in matters connected with wealth would ensure that labour and capital would seek the most profitable employments open to them. If a particular country have decided advantages in the production of food and raw material, it is better to leave labour and capital free to engage in these branches of production. By so doing, the country will have a surplus of food, &c., for exportation, by means of which she can purchase from other countries the manufactured goods she needs. In this way the country will get her manufactured goods cheaper, and her people will have the enjoyment of a larger aggregate of wealth than if she had used her labour and capital in the manufacture of goods which could be produced at less cost in other countries. Every artificial restriction by which labour and capital are forced into a channel which in a state of freedom they would not have sought, is a dead loss to the country. The great principle to be applied in such cases is the principle of *laissez faire*. Let things alone, and the self-interest of men will secure that both labour and capital will take the course which will lead to the greatest aggregate production of wealth. Take a particular example. The manufacture of cutlery, let us assume, is protected in the United States. If Protection be necessary to keep up the manufacture, that must be because cutlery is produced in America at a greater cost than in some other country. If now, the protective tariff were taken off, the manufacture of cutlery would cease, but the labour and capital hitherto employed in that industry would be set free for more profitable uses. The same amount of labour and capital would, in a country like America, produce an amount of food and raw material which would suffice to purchase from England or elsewhere the cutlery hitherto manufactured at home, and leave a surplus. This surplus is the measure of what the country loses, economically speaking, by protecting the particular industry in question.

A further application of the principle now being considered is to be found in the argument which says that Protection is in effect a tax on the many for the benefit of the few. To recur to the instance just given: the cutlery which is made by the protected home manufacture costs more than the cutlery which would have been imported under a system of Free Trade. Thus, everyone in America who has need of cutlery is in effect taxed for the benefit of the comparatively few persons engaged in the manufacture. Yet another application of the same leading principle is the familiar argument that it is for the interest of every country to "buy in the cheapest and sell in the dearest market."

The second of the two leading principles above stated is relied on by the Free Traders as furnishing a conclusive answer to a class of arguments not unfrequently used by the advocates of Protection. "Every nation which buys," says Professor Price, "sells also, and sells to the full value of what it buys." Of the principle thus explained he adds: " This is the first absolute, incontestable truth on which Free Trade reposes."* The principle has a double application, according as we look at the question from the standpoint of the producer, or from that of the consumer. Looking at the question from the producer's standpoint, and having in view the necessity of keeping the people productively employed, the principle is applied somewhat in this way. Free Trade, we are told,† cannot result in leaving people unemployed, because

---

* Chapters &c., p. 305.

† The reader will please bear in mind that I am now merely stating, as fairly as 1 can, the arguments of the Free Traders : I must not, of course, be taken as admitting the validity of the arguments thus stated. Indeed, this way of proving that Free Trade cannot injure the people of a country, whether viewed as producers or consumers, is a curious instance of the process known to logicians as arguing in a circle. It

the goods imported must be paid for by the exported goods ; and as these exported goods must be produced by labour, the goods that are imported really represent as much " home industry " as if they had been produced in the country. Looking at the question from the standpoint of the consumer, the principle now under consideration is relied on as showing that Free Trade can never operate as a drain upon the consumable wealth of a country. Commodities are paid for in commodities, and therefore as much wealth as is taken from a country in exports will come back to her in imports. The aggregate of wealth available for the consumption of her people cannot be diminished, and, for the reason already explained, will be increased.*

The foregoing is a brief statement of the case for universal Free Trade, as I understand it. I don't mean to say that I have stated every argument relied on by the Free Traders. But I have stated, and briefly explained the application of the two great principles upon which their case rests. The arguments on this side have been given so often and by so many writers

assumes throughout that the aggregate production and consumption of wealth in the country continues as great under Free Trade as under Protection ; which is in fact begging the whole question.

* The principle that " commodities are paid for in commodities," is also relied on as answering the argument that Free Trade may operate to drain a country of money. But as I am quite prepared to surrender that argument to the Free Traders, I have not thought it necessary to make the answer to it a part of my statement of the case for Free Trade.

that the reader will have little difficulty in ascertaining for himself whether or not my summary of the case for Free Trade is a fair one.

The next step will be to examine how far the arguments really prove the conclusions which they are commonly supposed to prove. Before we proceed to do this there is a preliminary question which needs to be made clear.

When Political Economists speak of the economic advantages which would result from universal Free Trade, are they looking at the question from a cosmopolitan or from a national standpoint? The distinction is a very important one, but is not always kept clearly in view. Take, for instance, the case of America and England. When English Free Traders assert that Free Trade with England is an enonomically sound policy for America, do they mean that Free Trade between the two countries would make America a wealthier country, or only that it would result in augmenting the aggregate wealth of England and America taken together? Political Economists are very fond of telling us that their science is strictly cosmopolitan. "Political Economy," says Mr. Lowe, "belongs to no na·tion—it is of no country." Speaking of the farms of Western America, Professor Bonamy Price observes, "I call them emphatically English fields, because Political Economy knows nothing about political divisions." This is all very well in theory; but if Political Economy really "knows nothing about political divisions," I fear it will have to learn something about these divisions before it can hope to better its present position. Assume it to be true that Free Trade between England and America would increase the aggregate production of wealth in the world. The American statesman wants to know something more than this before he consents to give Free Trade. He wants to be satisfied that the result will be to increase the wealth of the United States. If the aggregate increase were to take the form of a diminution in the wealth of the United States, accompanied by a more than corresponding increase in the wealth of England,* I fear that the cosmopolitan argument would not have much effect upon the Americans. In matters of this kind, it is a melancholy fact that American, French, and German statesmen all care a great deal about "political divisions;" and, for that matter, I think it would not be doing a very grievous injustice to English statesmen to affirm that they do the same.

We often hear it objected by Free Traders that if you are to protect one particular country against others, why not protect one part of the same country against the rest? If it be expedient that manufactures should be artificially created in France by protecting against England, why should not manufactures be created in Devonshire by protecting against Lan-

---

* We shall see further on that the argument that "Commodities are paid for in Commodities" does not really preclude this possibility.

cashire ? This objection illustrates very well the force
of the explanation which I am now making. The
primary duty of English statesmen is to forward the
interests of England as a whole : the interests of each
particular county of England are to be attended to
also, but are to be made subordinate to the interests
of the entire kingdom. If it were the primary duty of
French statesmen to forward the interests of England
and France, considered together as an aggregate
whole, and to subordinate to this the separate interests of France, then the objection just referred to
might have some force.* At present, however, this is
not the view of duty taken by the statesmen of various countries, including England. The view which is
taken may be regarded by some philanthropists as
narrow-minded and selfish. But the fact that this
view of public duty prevails is a fact which, I think,
we can hardly afford to ignore, in considering the
practical bearings of the Free Trade question. So,
again, in the case of Ireland, it is impossible to ade-
quately discuss the Free Trade question without
bringing in the national question in some shape or
other. If Ireland is to be regarded as a county, or
collection of counties, of England, then the question
of protecting Irish manufactures against English competition can hardly arise. But if Ireland ever suc-

---

* I say "might have," because I believe there are other respects in
which the analogy fails. But for the purpose of my present argument
the distinction above pointed out is sufficient.

ceeds in obtaining the right of making her own laws,
and regulating her own tariffs, then the expediency of
protecting her native industries will be one of the most
important questions which her legislators will have to
consider.

Even viewing the matter from a strictly cosmopolitan standpoint, a good deal might be said about
the enormous waste of human labour which takes
place in the process of carrying cotton from America
to Manchester, and then carrying back the manufactured article to America.   Something might also be
said in support of the proposition that a policy which
tends to distribute the aggregate wealth more evenly
amongst the various countries, is likely, in the long
run, to prove more beneficial to all than a policy which
renders possible and encourages the centralization of
wealth in particular countries.   But I do not propose
here to argue the question from a cosmopolitan standpoint.   Economists are confident that they can prove
that the result of universal Free Trade must be to
increase the aggregate production of wealth in the
world.   I do not believe that they do or can prove
even so much, but I am not at present concerned to
justify my belief in this respect.   The practical question is,—and so long as the division of the earth's
population into nations exists,—the practical question
will always be, how is Free Trade likely to affect particular countries?   In the following remarks, the problem is viewed from a strictly national standpoint.

With this explanation, we may proceed to examine the Free Trade arguments. The first argument, as we have seen, amounts shortly to this :—Protection has the effect of attracting to the protected industry labour and capital which would otherwise be more profitably employed. Hence the country loses by at least the difference between the productiveness of the labour and capital in the protected industry and the productiveness of the same labour and capital if left free to employ themselves more profitably. Every country has certain natural advantages. It is best she should produce the things with regard to the production of which she is most favourably situated. Free Trade is the law of nature. Protection is an artificial system devised by the perverted ingenuity of man to frustrate the beneficent designs of the Creator.

It may be at once admitted that this principle, like most of the laws of the Current Economy, has a certain amount of truth in it. It is a statement of one cause which, if a great many other causes were out of the way, would be the sole element in determining the solution of a particular problem. If there were no such things as national distinctions, and if the circulation of labour and capital from employment to employment were perfectly free all the world over, and if there were no such thing in production as the out-weighing of natural advantages by acquired advantages—if, in a word, the actual state of things were wholly different from what it is, then possibly the principle of *laissez faire* might safely be left to regulate the exchanges of the world. Even as things are, it would, no doubt, be possible to put extreme cases in which the consideration of natural advantages is strong enough to outweigh all others. Thus, when Adam Smith asks—" Would it be a reasonable law to prohibit the importation of all foreign wines merely to encourage the making of claret and burgundy in Scotland ?"*—the answer is obvious enough. But a very little consideration will show how far it is from being the fact that, as things are in the world, the effect of unrestricted Free Trade would be to cause the various kinds of wealth to be produced in the countries having the greatest natural advantages. Is it in accordance with the law of natural advantages that the cotton which is grown in the southern States of the Union should be carried several thousand miles across the ocean to be manufactured in England, and that then the manufactured articles should be carried back again across the ocean to be worn by the people of the country in which the raw material is produced? Is it in accordance with the law of natural advantages that the rails required for the making of American railways should be made in and imported from England, while the iron mines of America are as rich as any in the world ? Yet these, and such as these, are the results which take place at present to a very considerable extent in spite of the tariffs which America

* Wealth of Nations, book iv., chap. 2,

levies on English-made goods, and which would take place to a much greater extent if only the Free Traders could have their will. These considerations may suffice to show how very far they are from seeing to the bottom of the question who tell us triumphantly that the wisest policy is to allow every kind of wealth to be produced in the country having the greatest natural advantages for the production of that particular kind of wealth, and that *therefore* Free Trade is the policy which every country should pursue.

The truth is that the whole of this argument as to the unwisdom of artificially diverting labour and capital from a more productive to a less productive employment is based upon an assumption which is contrary to the facts of history. The whole argument obviously depends for its validity upon the assumption that the capital and labour employed in the protected manufactures would, in a state of Free Trade, be more productively employed. Negative this assumption and the whole superstructure of argument built upon it falls to pieces. The Free Traders assume that if it be once granted that a particular industry cannot be carried on in a country without Protection, it necessarily follows that in the country in question opportunities exist of more profitably employing the labour and capital which, by Protection, are attracted to the favoured industry. I cannot see that the conclusion follows from the premiss, and I assert that experience proves that the conclusion is often contrary to the fact. Take, for instance, the past history of this country. When those industries, which during the last century arose in Ireland in spite of every difficulty and discouragement, were finally killed by Free Trade with England, what became of the labour which had been employed therein? According to the theory of the Free Traders, it ought to have turned itself to more productive employments. However, the fact was that the only employment open to it was already overstocked, and that it was obliged either to stay in the country doing nothing, or to go and seek employment elsewhere. Let us, in imagination, reverse the process. Suppose a heavy tariff were now put upon the importation of woollen fabrics into Ireland;—or rather suppose that the importation was absolutely prohibited. What would be the effect of this? The main effect would be that a certain amount of labour which is now wasted, or nearly wasted, would be employed in producing woollen fabrics. True, these woollen goods would at first cost more to the consumer than similar goods imported from England. But this loss would be far more than counterbalanced by the gain to the community resulting from the productive employment of labour which would otherwise go to waste. And the farmers themselves, while for a time they might lose in their character of consumers of woollen goods, would gain in their character of producers of food. The creation of a prosperous home market for their produce would be a direct benefit to them. The question here is not, as the Free Traders would have us believe, whether a certain amount of labour and capital shall be employed in manufacturing woollen goods or be more profitably employed in some other way. The question is, which is better for the community—(1) that the labour and capital should be employed in the protected manufacture ; or (2), that the labour should remain idle or leave the country, and the capital cease to exist.

"But," the English Free Trader will say, "if your labour is wasted, that is your own fault. We never pretended that Free Trade could make a lazy people work. If your manufacturers have all died out, and if your people are thrown on the land as their sole means of livelihood, why is this? It is a long time now since all unfair laws directed against your manufactures have been removed. You have been put upon a footing of equality with England in every respect, and what was there to prevent you from starting manufactures of your own, excepting only the want of the necessary industry and enterprise?" This argument has been used more than once. It looks plausible enough, but it will hardly stand a close examination. In the first place, is it true that the Irish are a people essentially lazy and averse to work? I am very far from contending that the Irish are a perfect people, and I certainly do not hold the doctrine that the peasantry of this country is "the finest peasantry in the world." The Irish have many of the

faults one would expect to find in a people that have
been down-trodden and oppressed for centuries.
Under the circumstances, it would be very strange if
they had not.*   But I do not think that amongst their
faults is to be found an unwillingness to work hard
when they get fair wages.   Employers of labour in
the United States will tell you as a rule that they find
their Irish hands as hard-working as any others.   The
true reason why so many Irishmen are idle in Ireland
was seen clearly enough by Dean Swift.   " We are
apt," said the Dean, " to charge the Irish with laziness
because we seldom find them employed ; but we don't
consider that they have nothing to do."

There is no need to calumniate the Irish people, or
to make them seem worse than they really are in
order to account for the absence of manufactures in
Ireland.   While England was building up her great
manufacturing industry, the growth of manufactures
in Ireland was prevented by laws passed expressly
and avowedly with that object.   Then, when England

---

* This concession would by no means satisfy the able author of
"What Science is saying about Ireland?"   According to him the
"aboriginal Celt" is "prognathous," and the Lord knows what besides.   This is, no doubt, a very convenient way of shifting the blame
to the law of evolution, or whatever other agency the learned author
regards as the cause of race distinctions.   But how about the fact that
the "aboriginal Celt," when he was left to himself, and before the
Dane or the Norman came to interfere with him, was, in point of
learning and civilisation, considerably ahead of the other peoples of
Europe ?

had got a decisive start, when her manufactures were firmly established, and she had complete control of the market, Ireland was " put on a footing of perfect equality." The result was such as might have been, and probably was foreseen. A great accumulation of capital, an efficiency of labour enormously increased as well by that minute division of employments which a large capital permits as by the extensive use of labour-saving machinery, an abundance of skilled labour in various departments of manufacture, the tendency to increased centralisation in industrial production which has arisen with the increased facility of transfer and the more extensive use of costly machinery—these were amongst the advantages which were on the side of England. Nothing short of a miracle could have enabled Ireland, under such circumstances, to have developed any great manufacturing industry, so long as the English producers had free access to her markets. As Mr. Mill observes, " the superiority of one country over another in a branch of production often arises only from having begun it sooner."* Every kind of advantage that can be gained by " beginning sooner" had been gained by England before Ireland was " put on a footing of perfect equality."

I have dwelt at some length on the case of Ireland, because it seems to me to afford a very striking ex-

---

* Principles &c., book v., chap. x., sec. 1.

ample—perhaps the most striking example that could be adduced—of a state of circumstances in which the fundamental assumption of the Free Traders has proved to be directly contrary to the fact.

In the case of new countries with great natural advantages and comparatively sparse population, the fallacy involved in the argument we are considering is not so obvious. It is said that, in the case of such a country as the United States, the labour and capital which are, under a restrictive tariff, directed to the protected industries, could not fail, were Free Trade established, to find a more productive use. The assertion is plausible, and is not easily refuted. Yet, when the matter is examined into, the result is by no means so clear as the Free Traders would have us believe. Suppose that all the manufacturing industries of the United States were killed by Free Trade,* and that all the labour now employed in those indus-

---

* I don't mean to say that Free Trade would produce such a sweeping result. But that it would go a long way in this direction there can, I think, be little doubt. I say this, although I am aware that English Free Traders, finding their old arguments still without effect, have of late taken to showing that Free Trade would not, to any serious extent, affect injuriously the industries of the United States. I have no doubt the time will come when the United States will, with perfect Free Trade, be able to hold her ground, not only in her own markets but in foreign markets also. But as long as the price of labour is so much higher in America than in England, I cannot see how American manufacturers are to hold their own in open market against English competitors, notwithstanding the arguments of Professor Cairnes, Professor Fawcett, and others.

tries were thrown on the land, what would be the result? The result, according to the Free Traders,
would be that the production of food and raw material
would be increased in proportion to the additional
quantity of labour and capital now free to devote
themselves to that kind of production. It is by no
means certain that this would be the case, even in
such a country as the United States. But assume
that it would. The home market for bread-stuffs,
constituted by the industrial population who are consumers but not producers of this class of wealth, is at
the same time destroyed. The surplus, therefore, of
food and raw material available for exportation would
be largely increased. But as things now are, the
surplus of food, which America has available for the
supply of the foreign market, is very large, and is
generally in excess of the demand. Moreover, the
demand of Europe for American bread-stuffs is most
uncertain, and varies enormously from year to year.
If all the labourers of America were producers of food,
they would be under the necessity of trying to force
their great surplus upon European consumers, by
offering it at any price they could get. The value of
food and raw material relatively to manufactured
goods would be depressed. Thus, even if we assume
an increase in the production of bread-stuffs propor-
tionate to the labour set free by the destruction of the
protected industries, it by no means follows that the
aggregate production of wealth would be greater, if

we take into account the exchange value of the wealth produced. The contrary would probably be the case.

To reduce the people of a country to the dead level of a single industry, such as agriculture, has indirect as well as direct effects upon their material wealth. A brief reference has already been made to the various ways in which the growth of a diversified industry operates to promote the social development of a people. Will it be said that causes which tend to shape and determine the national character have got nothing to say to the national wealth? The American people have developed an extraordinary aptitude for mechanical invention; and the ingenuity used in devising labour-saving machinery has certainly tended very materially to increase the production of wealth in the United States. Suppose that America had never protected her industries and had allowed her people, like the Irish people, to be thrown entirely upon the land, what field would there have been for the employment of this inventive skill? Only the very limited one afforded by agricultural machinery. This is only one example of what is constantly occurring in other forms. The diversity of industry promotes individuality and variety of character, and helps to keep all the people of a country employed. It does all this because it enables each variety of faculty or taste to select the occupation which suits it best.

The foregoing considerations will suggest the true answer to that application of the argument now being

examined, which says that Protection is a tax upon the
many for the benefit of the few. The Cobden Club has of
late been making strenuous efforts to awaken the Western farmers of America to a sense of their forlorn condition. Some two years since a pamphlet was written
by a distinguished member of the Cobden Club and
addressed to the Western farmers of America. In this
pamphlet it was pointed out that the effect of Protection was to make the farmers pay much more for
their clothes and agricultural implements than they
would have to pay with Free Trade. Figures were
given, and the thing was made as clear as a sum in
simple arithmetic. What Protection was really doing
for the farmers was this : they were paying an annual
subsidy of $400,000,000 to the manufacturers of
Pennsylvania and New England. And the worst of
it was that the subsidy did not really benefit the
Eastern States in the least. It was so much wealth
thrown into the sea. It was the measure of the loss
which the community suffered by artificially forcing
labour and capital from more productive to less productive channels of employment. I remember reading
portions of this pamphlet for an intelligent farmer in one
of the Western States and being a good deal amused by
his reception of it. The arithmetic seemed unanswer-
able; but the farmer evidently had a shrewd suspicion
that there was a screw loose in the argument somewhere.
The conclusions which seem to be proved so clearly are
in truth arrived at by contemplating the farmer, from a

strictly abstract point of view, as "the consumer."
The average Western farmer is quite intelligent enough
to perceive that, if he has interests as a consumer, he
has also interests as a producer. If the cost of producing bread-stuffs were lowered by means of cheap
labour, cheap clothes, and cheap farm implements,
free competition and the necessity of forcing the produce on the European market would bring down the
price of the product in proportion, and the farmer would,
at best, be no better off than before.

Mr. Mongredien will find it hard to persuade the
Western farmers that it would be for their interest that
the manufacturing population of Pennsylvania and
New England should be driven on the land, and that
the home market at present existing in the Eastern
States for the farm produce of the West should be
destroyed.

We may now proceed to consider the second great
principle upon which the case for universal Free Trade
is grounded—the principle that commodities are paid
for in commodities ; that a country cannot continue for
any length of time to export more than she imports, or
to import more than she exports. We have already
seen that this proposition, even if strictly true, does not
by any means bear out all the conclusions which it is
commonly supposed to prove.*   A country may go on
exporting as much as it imports, and yet both exports

* See note to page 145.

and imports may rapidly diminish. Moreover, it must be remembered that the foreign trade of a country is by no means so sure a test of its real prosperity as English Economists sometimes assume. A policy which aims at creating a diversity of industry will tend, in so far as it is successful, to cause a country to carry on her exchanges within her own borders. It might conceivably happen in the case of such a country as the United States that the adoption of a Free Trade policy would largely increase the foreign trade, and yet would largely diminish the production of wealth, and impair the general prosperity of the country. It is then obvious that there is no inconsistency in giving the fullest assent to the proposition, that international trade is really an interchange of commodities, and at the same time holding that Free Trade may, under certain circumstances, affect very injuriously the wealth of a country.*

The principle we are now considering does certainly afford an answer to the argument that Free Trade may injure a country by permanently draining it of money. I admit that Adam Smith's refutation of the Mercantile Theory is tolerably conclusive. Yet it does not seem quite clear that the temporary drain of money which an adverse balance of trade may admit-

---

* For a striking instance of the way in which Free Traders beg the question in their application of the argument that "commodities are paid for in commodities," see Mr. Mongredien's "Pleas for Protection Examined," pp. 17, 18, and 19.

tedly cause, may not prove a very serious inconvenience to the country from which it takes place. But, as already intimated, I am willing to give up the "drain of money" argument altogether. Free Traders are entitled to the credit of having, to a great extent, disposed of it, and I think that the case for Protection, to the extent here advocated, can very easily dispense with it.

There is one other conclusion of importance which the principle that "commodities are paid for in commodities" would, if strictly true, justify. It would show that one country could not continue under a system of Free Trade to appropriate and consume the wealth of another country without returning full value therefor. If this were true, while it would by no means be sufficient to prove the case for Free Trade, it would certainly negative a formidable argument on the other side. Let us see what are the facts.

I have already observed that Mr. Farrer's anxiety to extinguish the Fair Traders betrays him into using some arguments which sound strange as coming from an advocate of universal Free Trade. In the 26th chapter of his pamphlet he calls attention to the fact, now pretty generally known, that of recent years the imports of England have enormously exceeded her exports.* The statistics of exports and imports for

---

* In alluding to this subject it is right to say that, as Mr. Farrer points out, these statistics are apt to mislead, unless used with great care. A similar caution is given by Mr. Giffen in his recent pamphlet

1880 show that in that year alone the imports of England exceeded her exports by £124,815,099. How is this explained? In his 13th chapter, Mr. Farrer disposes of some very absurd arguments which the Fair Traders base upon this excess of imports over exports. When eminent politicians argue as though it were a serious economic loss to England to be able to absorb each year commodities to the value of over one hundred millions sterling without giving anything in exchange therefor, one is tempted to ask, "are these men in earnest, or are they deliberately trading upon the gullibility of their fellow-men?" The explanation of the phenomenon given by Mr. Farrer is the obvious and the true one. It is not strictly true that commodities are always paid for in commodities. It is quite possible that a country may, for a long time, continue to steadily export more than she imports, and may leave the unpaid balance outstanding upon securities of some kind in the country to which she is exporting. When in this way a large debt has been

on "The Use of Import and Export Statistics." But even assuming that the excess of imports over exports, more especially as regards the United States, is capable of being, to some extent, explained in the ways suggested by Mr. Giffen (pp. 18-19, and p. 26, *et seq.*), that does not weaken, but rather strengthens the above argument. Both Mr. Farrer and Mr. Giffen admit that England has " enormous investments abroad;" and Mr. Giffen's explanation of the statistics simply goes to show, as he himself points out (p. 40), that the real excess of imports is not sufficient to pay the interest, and hence that the debt itself is increasing every day.

created, it will be possible for the creditor country to go on for an indefinite time to come importing from the debtor country a greater quantity of wealth than she exports—the balance going to pay the interest upon the debt. This is precisely the process that England has been carrying on since she has succeeded in establishing her position as the workshop of the world.   The total of British foreign investments has been, Mr. Farrer tells us, "estimated by competent statisticians at from £1,500,000,000 to £2,000,000,000." The excess of imports over exports during 1880 would be more than sufficient to pay the interest even upon this enormous debt; but Mr. Farrer is at some pains to show that there are other causes which fully account for the surplus, so as to negative the suggestion that any portion thereof goes to pay off the principal of the debt.   What does all this amount to?   It amounts to saying that up to the present England's manufacturing supremacy has been such as to enable her, in spite of the tariffs imposed upon her goods by foreign countries, to levy upon the rest of the world a permanent annual tribute of over one hundred millions sterling.

In an address recently delivered in Dublin, Mr. Goldwin Smith triumphantly observed: "The accumulated wealth of England is prodigious; she is the grand investor; all other countries are mortgaged to her, and, like a rich man living on his patrimony, she can afford to buy more than she sells."   All very well for England, but not quite so well for the countries that are mortgaged.

The argument derived from the excess of British imports applies with peculiar force to the case of the United States. It appears from the tables at the end of Mr. Farrer's pamphlet that the total money value of the exports from Great Britain to the United States, during the year 1880, was £37,954,000; while the money value of the imports from the States to Great Britain, during the same year, was £107,081,000; so that, of the one hundred millions which England absorbed during the year without giving anything in return for it, it would seem that close upon £70,000,000 came from the United States.* Again, if we take the five years ending with 1880, we find that, according to Mr. Farrer, the exports to the United States during this period amounted to £121,118,000, and the imports from the United States during the same period amounted to £441,770,000; showing that during this period of five years England has taken from the United States alone wealth to the value of £320,652,000, without giving anything in return therefor. This is a somewhat startling comment upon the doctrine that " commodities are paid for in commodities," and that in a trade between two countries the exports and imports must balance one another.

* As to the ways in which this excess has been in part explained, see note to page 164. English Free Traders are not, of course, igno-

But it will be said, America has had her turn. If she is giving more than she receives now, that is simply because she had previously been receiving more than she gave. The surplus which she now pays is only the interest upon capital which England has lent to her, and of which she has had the benefit. America, therefore, has no cause to complain. Certainly, in one sense, America has no cause to complain. England has done nothing which America would not have done to England had she been able. But it does not follow from this that the process may not in the long run prove very injurious to the United States. The leading English Economists explain very clearly the way in which the capital of a country is constantly being consumed, and kept up by reproduction. This fact, they tell us, explains how it may happen that a country which has been devastated by a great war may, in a suprisingly short time, be as wealthy as ever : while, on the other hand, a country into which a great quantity of wealth has suddenly been poured, may, in a very few years, be none the richer. We have recently seen both statements receive a striking illustration in the case of France and Germany. These considerations show how far it is from being the fact that the benefit which a country derives from having the use of a large quantity of capital necessarily and permanently balances the loss she suffers by having to pay the rant of the fact, that the imports of a country may permanently exceed its exports in the way above described. But they treat this as a fact of trifling importance which does not affect their arguments.

interest. It may happen, and it often does happen, that at the end of a few years the borrowing country is none the richer for the loan, and that the simple effect of the whole transaction is to saddle the one country with the payment of a permanent tribute to the other. No doubt it can hardly be said that this has, so far, been the only effect of the transaction in the United States. The influx of English capital has probably contributed very materially to promote the wonderfully rapid development of the Western States. Whether this result be an unmixed good is very open to question. But assume that it is so. It by no means follows that the good may not, in the long run, prove to have been too dearly bought. Recent statistics go to show that, so far from the great surplus of American exports to England having in part gone to clear off the capital debt, it has, in truth, been not sufficient to meet the interest, and that the debt is still increasing.* There seems every reason to expect that, if things go on as at present, the United States will, before very long, be·under tribute to England to the extent of £100,000,000 per annum. Even for so vast a country as the Union, this is a very serious prospect. And if,,in spite of the protective tariff, England has already been able to lay America under contribution to the extent of close upon £70,000,000 per annum, it is hard to say what the amount of the tribute might have been had the English manufacturers had free access to the American markets.

* As to this, see further note to page 164.

We have now examined the chief applications of the two great principles upon which the Free Traders rely. We have seen that the Free Trade arguments are far from being as conclusive as Professor Bonamy Price and others would have us believe. The result of our examination goes rather to show that in certain cases the balance of argument is strongly against Free Trade. If a country whose industrial development is in a backward stage, throws open its markets to the free competition of another country far ahead of it in all the essentials of cheap production, the necessary result will be to more or less entirely kill out the manufactures of the backward country and check the growth of a varied industry. For a country so situated the wise course would seem to be not a policy of cosmopolitan Free Trade, but a policy of national Protection.*

4. It only remains now to say a few words upon

---

* In closing this examination of the Free Trade arguments it is fair to state that several of the pleas for Protection which I have incidentally mentioned have been already examined by leading Free Traders, and answered in a way which the writers very evidently regard as conclusive. Not being able myself to regard the answers as by any means conclusive, I would ask the reader to look into Professor Fawcett's " Free Trade and Protection " (see in particular chap. iv.), or Mr. Mongredien's " Pleas for Protection Examined," and judge for himself. I may add that, though I have been incidentally led to state some of the arguments for Protection, and to give my own opinion as to the result, the reader must not suppose that I purport to give a complete statement of the case for Protection. The arguments on that side will be found in Professor Thompson's book; some of the leading

the historical aspect of the question. In the first
chapter of this book reference was made to the fact
that in the principal countries of the world, excepting
England, the tendency of late years has been towards
Protection. I must confess I am so far a believer in
the superiority of practice over theory as to attach
considerable importance to this fact. It is all very well
to say that the people of a country are hood-winked
by a few capitalists who have an interest in maintaining Protection. But, when we see a statesman like
Prince Bismarck deliberately returning to a policy of
Protection after giving a fair trial to a policy of comparative Free Trade, the significance of this result is not
to be so easily explained away. The statesmen who
carry on the government of France and Germany, of
the United States, and of Canada, may be presumed
to be not wholly ignorant of the favourite arguments
of the Free Traders. English Economists are very
severe upon those who meet their arguments by
"suggestions of the superior wisdom of Prince Bismarck or M. Thiers." Yet, as already intimated, I am
sufficiently perverse to attach much weight to such
suggestions, notwithstanding Mr. Farrer's contempt
for them. When I see such statesmen as M. Thiers
and Prince Bismarck, having vast practical experience
and exceptional opportunities of observing results,

arguments are also clearly stated and explained in an article on " Free
Trade from an American Standpoint," by Albert J. Leffingwell, in the
Contemporary Review for July, 1880.

declaring themselves in favour of a Protective policy, that fact alone would, in my mind, outweigh a good deal of *a priori* reasoning in favour of universal Free Trade. If it be true, as Professor Price and others seem to think, that the advantages of Free Trade under all circumstances are as clearly provable as the principles of the multiplication table or the propositions of Euclid, the necessary inference is that the statesmen who guide the destinies of the protective nations are either fools or the worst kind of knaves. The *a priori* proof should be much more conclusive than it is, before I would let myself be coerced to any such conclusion.

I do not propose here going into any detailed examination of the historical evidence in the various countries. The reader who cares to pursue this branch of the subject for himself, will find an excellent summary of the historical argument for Protection in the twelfth chapter of Professor Thompson's " Social Science and National Economy." It is possible, no doubt, that Professor Thompson's view of history may be to some extent the result of the influences which surround him. He quotes against the English writers the maxim, " Homines facile credunt id quod volunt." But this cuts two ways. It is only fair to remember that if the people of England have strong reason to desire Free Trade, the people of Pennsylvania have equally strong reason to desire Protection. Speaking of the student of Sociology, Mr. Herbert Spencer observes: "In his capacity of citizen, helped to live by the life of his society, embedded in its structures, sharing in its activities, breathing its atmosphere of thought and sentiment, he is partially coerced into such views as favour harmonious co-operation with his fellow-citizens."*   Something to a like effect might be said of the Political Economist.   Without in the least insinuating that the English Economists, any more than Professor Thompson, designedly teach a certain doctrine simply because it is popular, we may admit that they are both unconsciously influenced by the atmosphere in which they live.   But, making every allowance for this consideration, it still seems to me that Professor Thompson makes out a very strong case for Protection on historical grounds.   I am not aware that the Free Traders have ever even attempted to make out a like case for Free Trade.   Of course we have frequently heard accounts of the great prosperity of England since she adopted Free Trade. But, as already observed, that proves nothing more than that England had then reached the stage of industrial development at which Free Trade becomes a sound policy.   She took good care not to adopt Free Trade until she had reached that stage, and reached it by a long-continued policy of strict Protection.

Professor Thompson, in the chapter just referred to, briefly examines the bearing of the historical evi-

* Study of Sociology, 3rd ed., p. 386.

dence upon the Free Trade controversy in the cases of the following countries—France, England, Canada, Australia, Ireland, India, Belgium, Germany, Russia, Sweden and Denmark, Spain, Portugal, Turkey, and the United States. Of European countries, with one exception, I do not propose to say anything here. It may be that, in the case of France and Germany, the historical evidence is not quite so entirely on one side as Professor Thompson supposes. France and Germany are probably approaching the stage at which Protection ceases to be necessary. But in the case of countries like these, where the abstract arguments for and against Free Trade appear to be nearly evenly balanced, one is all the more inclined to accept as conclusive the decisions of statesmen whose knowledge of the countries in question is exceptional, and whose capacity and patriotism are not denied.

In a recent article in the Fortnightly Review,* Mr. Baden-Powell founds an argument for Free Trade upon an examination of the case of Victoria and New South Wales. Victoria, he tells us, has had, since 1871, an "intensified form of Protection;" while New South Wales has, during the same period, "followed an essentially Free Trade course." He then gives a variety of facts and figures tending to show that New South Wales has done better with Free Trade than Victoria has done with Protection. If Mr. Baden-

* See the number for March, 1882.

Powell has told us the whole truth, and if his facts really justify his conclusions, he has certainly made out a very telling argument for Free Trade. He has produced the one solitary case, so far as I am aware, in which the historical argument in the case of young communities favours absolute Free Trade. I do not know enough about Australia to be able to argue the question out. But there are one or two obvious considerations which induce me to regard Mr. Baden-Powell's argument with suspicion. In the first place, as to his facts. He says Victoria has had a " very intensified form" of Protection since 1871. This seems entirely at variance with Mr. Farrer's statements. " Victoria," says Mr. Farrer, " which had, in 1859, a tariff as low as New South Wales, has raised her duties considerably in 1879, and has raised them still more since. They are now considerable, and are on many important articles as high as those of France, Italy, or Austria, and higher than those of Holland or Norway."* It would seem, then, that according to Mr. Farrer, it would hardly be true even now to say that an "intensified form of Protection" prevails in Victoria ; and further, that such a degree of Protection as does prevail is the result rather of duties imposed at the end than at the beginning of the decade which Mr. Baden-Powell considers. One thing, at all events, seems certain, if Mr. Farrer's facts may be accepted

* Free Trade *v.* Fair Trade, chap. vi.

as correct. Not only in Victoria, but also in South Australia, Western Australia, Tasmania, and New Zealand, the tariffs were largely increased in 1879. This does not look as if the legislatures in these various colonies took the view which Mr. Baden-Powell takes regarding the lesson to be learned from the respective experiences, during the previous period, of Victoria and New South Wales. Let us assume, however, that Mr. Baden-Powell is correct in stating that during the decade ending in 1881 the policy of Victoria was strictly protective, while that of New South Wales was practically free trade. Let us further assume that he is right in saying that during the same period the progress and general prosperity of New South Wales was decidedly greater than that of Victoria. Before Mr. Baden-Powell is justified in concluding from these premises that the difference between the two colonies in prosperity and progress was necessarily the result of their different commercial policies, he must show that the colonies were otherwise similarly situated ; that there were not other causes which might be expected to bring about the very results which he dwells upon. Mr. Baden-Powell seems to be conscious that this is necessary to his argument. On the first page of his article he says :— " So far as the purpose in hand is concerned these two countries were, in the year 1870, sufficient counterparts of each other in regard to economic environments and opportunities." This is somewhat vague. The sentence, as explained by what follows, seems to amount to the expression of a belief that the circumstances of Victoria and New South Wales, in 1870, were in all other respects so similar that one is coerced to conclude that the difference in progress during the ensuing decade must have been caused by the difference in commercial policy. If this be really what Mr. Baden-Powell desires to convey, it certainly does not need any very profound knowledge of Australian history to prove that he is in error.

The history of Victoria, previous to 1870, is in many respects in strong contrast with that of New South Wales. The last-named colony is by much the oldest of the Australian settlements. It has had a comparatively slow but steady growth, and it has taken close upon a century to reach its present stage of development. Victoria, on the other hand, did not commence to exist as a separate colony till some thirty years ago. Down to the year 1850, the territory which is now known as Victoria formed a portion of the colony of New South Wales. Then came the discovery of gold early in 1851. The influx of gold-seekers was so great that in a few years the population of Victoria exceeded that of New South Wales. "The increase of population caused by the rush for gold was amazing. From 76,000, in 1850, it increased to 312,000 in 1856; to 538,000 in 1860, and to 760,000 in 1870."* These figures alone suffice to show under

* Wallace's "Australasia," p. 175.

13

what very exceptional circumstances the growth of
Victoria had proceeded up to the commencement of
the period which Mr. Baden-Powell examines. Such
an abnormally and almost morbidly rapid growth would
naturally produce a reaction.   Mr. Baden-Powell admits that during the period which he examines, some
20,000 labourers were thrown out of employment by
the failure of the gold industry.   The number is very
large for a country like Victoria.   Mr. Baden-Powell,
however, assumes, as indeed all English Free Traders
do, that if in any country labour be thrown out of employment by the failure of a particular industry, it can
always and immediately find some other employment
to which to "circulate." He is so far from seeing in the
partial failure of the gold industry of Victoria a reason
which may to some extent account for the depression
he notices, that he actually relies on that failure as a
circumstance in favour of Victoria.   The fact that
20,000 labourers were thrown out of work some time
between 1870 and 1880 is relied on as helping to prove
that the comparatively slow progress of Victoria during the decade cannot have been due to any cause
other than her commercial policy.   Mr. Baden-Powell
further admits that the quantity of unoccupied land in
New South Wales is much greater than in Victoria.
This is indeed sufficiently obvious.   In extent New
South Wales is nearly four times as large as Victoria,
while the population of Victoria is considerably larger
than that of New South Wales.   It may be said that

so long as each country has still a great quantity of land unoccupied, it can make little difference that the quantity of unoccupied land in the one country is greater than in the other. But we may safely presume that the best land has been taken up in Victoria, and probably we would not be far wrong if we said that nearly all the land has been taken up, which, as things now are in the colony, is worth taking up. At all events, we know as a fact, that about the very period at which Mr. Baden-Powell commences his examination, the land question in Victoria was passing through a crisis of great severity.

It thus appears that the most superficial examination of the history of New South Wales and of Victoria is sufficient to dispose of the assumption that their "economic environments and opportunities" were "practically similar." Not only did the circumstances of the two colonies differ very decidedly, but they differed in a way which would lead us to expect results of the kind described in Mr. Baden-Powell's paper. The one other country in the world which most resembles Victoria in its growth is the State of California. California, like Victoria, has had an abnormally rapid growth owing to the discovery of gold. In "Progress and Poverty"* Mr. Henry George describes a state of things as taking place in California very similar to that which, according to Mr. Baden-Powell, took place during the same period in Victoria. The severity of

* See book v., chap. i.

the reaction in California was probably mitigated to a great extent by the abundance of fertile land; but otherwise the phenomena appear to have been very much alike. The causes to which Mr. George attributes the state of things just referred to, are such as are sure to arise in any country whose growth has been abnormally rapid, wholly irrespective of any question of Free Trade or Protection. If we were to compare carefully the condition of California during the ten years previous to 1880 with that of some of the older States whose growth has been more gradual, it is more than likely that the comparison would give results similar to those arrived at in Mr. Baden-Powell's comparison of Victoria and New South Wales. It is hardly necessary to add that, as between California and the other States of the Union, the cause to which Mr. Baden-Powell attributes the difference between the two Australian colonies has no existence.

Mr. Baden-Powell prefaces his comparison with the following observation: "This is the first time in history that we meet with the story, told in the details of actual fact, of two communities growing up side by side with practically similar economic environments and opportunities, but pursuing the one a Free Trade and the other a Protectionist policy." Here again I venture to join issue with Mr. Baden-Powell upon a question of fact. There is at least one other instance in history of two communities "growing up side by side and pursuing the one a Free Trade and the other a Protectionist policy." The experiment in the case I am now referring to has been tried for a much longer period—a period long enough to make it impossible for us to attribute the difference of results to any temporary depression or reaction. A comparison of the present prosperity and past progress of the two countries I speak of yields results far more striking and far more conclusive than the comparison instituted by Mr. Baden-Powell. I need hardly say that I refer to the case of Canada and the United States.

In his book on "Social Science and National Economy," already so frequently cited, Professor Thompson gives a sketch of the history of the tariff question in the United States. This history may be briefly summed up as follows. Previous to the War of the Revolution the North American Colonies had a taste of the kind of Free Trade which England was at the same time conceding to Ireland. That is to say, while they were obliged to receive all kinds of manufactured goods from England free of duty, or subject only to very low duties, they were in many instances either absolutely or practically forbidden to export the products of their home industry, and in some cases the manufacture itself was prohibited and declared a "common nuisance." For some few years after the Revolution there was practically Free Trade between England and the States. Then came the tariff of 1790, accompanied by the famous "Treasury Report" of Secretary Hamilton. This report was certainly a very wonderful instance of statesmanlike sagacity and foresight. "It was a masterly statement of the new era upon which industry was entering, through the use of machinery and the division of labour; of the advantages that would be lost to the nation who fell behind in this advance; of the inter-dependence of all the material interests of the country; and of the relation of a diversified industry to national prosperity. It stated with candour and refuted with force the usual objections to a protective policy."* The tariff of 1790 has been described as mildly protective. The state of things established by this tariff may be said to have, in the main, prevailed from 1790 to 1824. There was an interval, during and prior to the war of 1812, when English goods were more rigidly excluded. In 1824, a tariff was enacted which was in the strictest sense protective. In 1828, the report of the then Secretary of the Treasury "called attention to the general prosperity that had followed the adoption of the tariff of 1824, and suggested an increase of some leading duties."† In pursuance of this recommendation a still more protective tariff was enacted. It is eminently worthy of note that, in the debate on the tariff of 1828, Daniel Webster declared himself a convert to the principle of Protec-

---

* Social Science &c., by Professor Thompson, p. 357.
† Id., p. 363-4.

tion.   In 1824, he had warmly opposed the tariff; but
it would seem that a short experience of the effects of
Protection sufficed to convert him.   In 1833, the leading
States of the South called for Free Trade and threatened
to secede if the tariff of 1828 were maintained.   A
compromise was effected, by which it was provided
that the duties should be gradually lowered.   For some
nine years the process of gradual lowering went on,
and, says Professor Thompson, "the gradual closing
of American factories and workshops went with it . . .
Labour ran begging for employment, and during 1839-
1841 the cry was heard far and near, 'Give me work!
only give me work!   Make your own terms; myself
and my family have nothing to eat!'"

At last the American people seem to have very generally come to the conclusion that they had had enough
of Free Trade experiments.   In 1842, a tariff was
enacted which was, in the fullest sense, protective.
The Southern States no longer spoke of secession.
The ruin of the industries of New England had not
seemingly benefited the Southern planters, as much as
they had expected.   In 1846, the duties were again
modified.   The Dallas tariff was enacted.   This tariff,
though considerably lower than that of 1842, was still
protective.   The commercial policy of the next eleven
years may be described as similar in its general features
to that which prevailed previous to 1824.   It was a policy
of mild Protection.   In 1857, the duties were reduced
25 per cent.—a more decided step in the direction of

absolute Free Trade than had been made since the
adoption of the tariff of 1790. This policy, however,
did not last long. In 1861 the great civil war began,
and shortly afterwards the "very intensified form of
Protection," known as the Morrill tariff, was enacted.
The Morrill tariff, with some slight modifications, has
been in force ever since, and there is every prospect
that it will remain in force for a considerable time to
come.

The prosperity and progress of the United States
under this policy of strict Protection has been just as
remarkable as the prosperity of England with Free
Trade. Professor Thompson shows clearly that the
advance in wealth and general prosperity of the United
States has been much more rapid in proportion since
the final adoption of strict Protection than during the
previous period.

To such readers as may not have time to study this
very interesting chapter of history for themselves, the
foregoing brief sketch may serve to give an idea of
the main outlines of the commercial policy of the
United States during the last one hundred years.
That policy may be summarised as follows :—It was a
policy of Protection, usually in a modified form, but
which, at times, became more stringent ; which was
varied now and then by brief experiments in the direction of Free Trade, and which some twenty years
since became and has since remained a policy of strict
Protection.

During the period we have been surveying a different policy was pursued by the country which adjoins the States upon the north. The commercial policy of ·Canada, down to the year 1879, was in the main a policy of Free Trade, modified by the imposition of what is known as " a tariff for revenue." Those who are familiar with the Free Trade controversy will be aware that a tariff for revenue is non-protective. Indeed, the least consideration shows that in proportion as a tariff becomes protective it ceases to yield a revenue. If the duties are too low to be protective, the goods will be imported and the duties will be paid. Raise the duties to such an extent as to practically prohibit importation, and you put an end to all revenue from this source. No goods are imported and no duty is paid. Now, the guiding principle of Canadian policy until recently was to make the import duties a source of revenue. In 1862, the Canadian Finance Minister was at some pains to assure the Manchester Chamber of Commerce that the commercial policy of Canada was in no sense protective. The reasons which Mr. Galt put forward as proving that the tariff of Canada was not protective, have a curious bearing upon a certain class of Free Trade arguments which have of late become common. " The best evidence," said Mr. Galt, " that could be offered against the charge of Protection was that the effect of the tariff had not been to produce manufactures. The manufactures of Canada were those that might be expected in a new country—nails, steam-engines, coarse woollens, and other articles necessary in a newly-settled country. There was not at that moment a single cotton mill in Canada nor a silk manufactory." There is something very amusing, and at the same time very instructive, in this idea of a Canadian minister defending his country before the Manchester Chamber of Commerce against the charge of having a cotton mill or a silk manufactory.*

Here, then, we have a very remarkable instance of "two young communities growing up side by side," and "pursuing, the one a Free Trade, the other a Protectionist policy:" and this not for a few years only but for a century. But, it may be objected, it cannot be said of these two countries that they had "practically similar economic environments and opportunities." I do not assert that the "economic environments and opportunities" of the two countries were in all respects alike. But I do assert that the difference in prosperity and progress is such as is not at all accounted for by any difference that may exist in natural advantages or opportunities. In this case, be it again observed, the contrast is totally different

* See Thompson's Social Science, &c., p. 303, and in further proof that the tariff of Canada was non-protective, see an article by Mr. Goldwin Smith in the Contemporary Review for September, 1881. Mr. Smith denies that the tariff is rendered protective even by the heavy increases of duties in 1879.

in kind from that dwelt on in Mr. Baden-Powell's comparison.   In the case of Victoria and New South Wales, the most that can be said is that the protective country, having for a time progressed much more rapidly than the free trade country, has of late been suffering from a depression, and has upon the whole not done so well as her neighbour during the last decade.   In the case of the United States and Canada, the obvious fact is that, after making every allowance for differences in natural advantages, the wealth and general prosperity of the protective country has been for a century, and is to-day, out of all proportion greater than that of the free trade country.

It seems to be very doubtful if the difference in natural advantages between Canada and the United States is at all as great as has been supposed.   The extent of fertile land is, no doubt, greater in the United States, but the quality seems to be at least as good in Canada.   It is the general belief in America, that along the greater portion of the frontier the advantage in fertility is on the British side.   It seems certain that the land of Upper Canada is, as a rule, very much superior in natural fertility to the land of the New England States.   The pioneer farmers of the Union had settled and brought into cultivation a large part, pro-bably the greater part, of the western lands available for agriculture, before the Canadians seemed to wake up to the fact that they, too, had in the West a vast extent of the finest wheat-growing land in the world.

Of the rapidity with which the Western States of the Union have been taken into cultivation, it has been said that "nothing in the history of the world has ever equalled the settling up of the vast territories of the North-West and of the Pacific sea-board."* Here, again, we observe that history furnishes a flat contradiction to the theory that in countries like America and Canada, Protection is prejudicial to the interests of the farming classes. In the rapidity with which the Western States of the Union have been settled, and in the fact that to-day the poor land of New England will fetch a higher price than the rich land of Upper Canada, we see strikingly exemplified the extent to which the industries of a country are mutually dependent upon one another. We see practical proof of the fact that the diversity of industry, which promotes general prosperity and national enterprise, advances the interest of each separate class of producers by advancing the interests of all taken together.

In comparing the wealth and progress of Canada and the United States there is no need of detailed statistics. The difference is, so to speak, of a wholesale kind. It is patent to the most superficial observer, whether his observation take the form of

---

* See an article by J. M. Farrer, in the Contemporary Review for August, 1881, p. 244. As already hinted, it may fairly be questioned whether the wonderfully rapid progress of the United States in this respect be an unmixed good. But the case made for Free Trade is that it promotes material progress. I am now meeting the Free Traders on their own ground.

glancing over the histories and statistics of the two countries, or of observing for himself the different appearances which they now present. Anyone who has been to the falls of Niagara cannot fail to have been struck by the contrast I am referring to. "On the American side all is activity and bustle." The men have too much to do, their time is too valuable, to make it worth their while to persecute tourists with offers of, "Show you the scenery, sir." Cross to the Canadian side, and you feel inclined to believe that you have suddenly been transported some thousands of miles to the eastward. The surroundings are just such as you may remember in some "show place" of the Old World, where the energies of the population seem to be mainly devoted to the trade of fleecing tourists.

Upwards of forty years ago, a famous report upon the state of Canada was submitted to the English Government by a very remarkable man. In the report I refer to, Lord Durham observes : "By describing one side of the frontier and reversing the picture the other would be described. On the American side all is activity and bustle. The forest has been widely cleared; every year. numerous settlements are formed, and thousands of farms are created out of the waste ; the country is intersected with common roads. . . . On the British side of the line, with the exception of a few favoured spots, where some approach to American prosperity is apparent, all seems waste and desolate.

. . . Throughout the frontier, from Amherstburgh to the ocean, the market value of land is much greater on the American than on the British side. In not a few parts, this difference amounts to a thousand per cent. . . . I am positively assured that superior natural fertility belongs to the British side. In Upper Canada, the whole of the great peninsula between Lakes Erie and Huron, comprising nearly half the available land of the province, is generally considered the best grain country of the American Continent. : . . I do not believe that the universal difference in the value of land can anywhere be fairly attributed to natural causes.* It is right to say that Lord Durham attributes the marked contrast which he describes to causes quite irrespective of any difference in commercial policy.† He suggests certain remedies, which remedies do not include Protection for the home industries of Canada.‡ The principal reforms urged by Lord Durham were carried out, shortly after the report was made. "Lord Durham's report began a new era ; its recommendations, extending to complete internal self-government, were in full operation in Canada within two or three years, and have since been extended to nearly all the other colonies of European

* "Report on the affairs of British North America," by the Earl of Durham, London, 1839, pp. 91, 92, 93. The above quotation is much abridged, but the entire passage is well worth reading.

† *Id.*, p. 24, *et seq.*

‡ *Id.*, p. 113, *et seq.*

race which have any claim to the character of important communities."*

I do not deny that the reforms advocated by Lord
Durham, and subsequently carried into effect, may
have caused a decided change for the better. But it
is a fact, patent to anyone who cares to observe it,
that the difference between the American and British
sides of the frontier, dwelt on in the Report, still
exists after forty years of home rule in Canada. The
difference may be less in degree, but in kind it is still
the same.

In such a case it is hardly necessary to give statistics.
Everyone knows that the population of the United
States has increased much faster than, and is at present
many times as great as that of Canada. As regards
the comparative wealth of the two countries one fact
may suffice. I find, from the tables at the end of Mr.
Farrer's pamphlet, that the exports from British
America to the United Kingdom during the five years
ending with 1880, were in value little more than one-
eighth of the exports from the United States during
the same period. During almost the whole of this
period there was practical Free Trade between England and Canada. During the same period the manufactures of the United States were strictly protected
against English competition. Protection, in checking
imports, checks exports also, and tends to cause a

* J. S. Mill, Autobiography, pp. 216, 217.

nation, so far as possible, to carry on her exchanges within her own borders. If we keep these facts in view, the above comparison between the exports from Canada and the exports from the United States may serve to give us a rough general idea of the comparative wealth of the two countries.

To the argument in favour of Protection in young communities, furnished by the history of the English-speaking peoples of North America, there is, so far as I can see, but one answer. Let the Free Traders show, if they can, that, apart from all questions of commercial policy, there have been differences in " economic environments and opportunities" sufficient to account for the enormous disparity between Canada and the United States in wealth and general progress. And they must even do something more than this; since, if their teachings were sound, the wealth of Canada ought to be much greater in proportion than that of the United States. Will English Economists say that the difference is due to the fact that the one country was an independent nation, while the other was only a colony of England? " Westward the course of empire takes its way," wrote Berkeley more than one hundred and thirty years ago. May it be that it was because of the provincialism of Canada that while the farmers of the Republic had their faces turned to the west, the face of the Canadian was still turned to the east? If English Economists affirm that this was one cause of the difference we have been dwelling on, I certainly will not deny that it was so. But I cannot allow that even this cause is sufficient to fully account for the phenomenon. There can be little doubt as to the lesson which the Canadians themselves have drawn from the comparison. They do not seem to be as yet tired of the suzerainty of England, but they are heartily sick of Free Trade with her. After having been deluged with Free Trade arguments, and after having had quite enough of Free Trade practice, the Canadians have at last began to suspect that in this matter Brother Jonathan is not quite such a fool as he is represented. I have been assured, with what amount of truth I cannot say, that the good results of the Canadian tariff of 1879 are already beginning to be apparent.

In the course of this chapter certain questions were stated as being, in the opinion of the present writer, still unanswered by the arguments of the Free Traders. If the reader will revert to these questions, he will find that they indicate a doubt as to the wisdom of a policy of Free Trade, not only in the case of young communities, with a sparse population and abundance of land, but also in the case of older and more thickly peopled countries whenever, owing to special circumstances, the industrial development of such countries is in a comparatively backward stage. We have just considered what is certainly the most striking example of the first class furnished by history. We may conclude this chapter with a brief reference to what is probably the most striking example of the second class.

I have already referred to the case of Ireland. I have
instanced it as furnishing a very remarkable example of
a case in which the labour and capital set free when
certain industries were killed by Free Trade, did *not*, as
a matter of fact, turn themselves to more productive
employments.   The industrial history of Ireland has a
very striking and a very instructive bearing upon the
Free Trade controversy.   The process by which the
infant manufactures of Ireland were deliberately destroyed is familiar to every student of Irish history.
During the last years of the seventeenth century and
during the entire of the eighteenth century, while England was building up her manufacturing supremacy, the
rising manufactures of Ireland were repressed by English-made laws.   These laws had at least the merit of
being outspoken. They were enacted avowedly for the
purpose of destroying the Irish manufactures, which
were, in several cases, like those of the American
colonies, declared to be a " common nuisance."

The story has been told so often that it is unneces-
sary for me to repeat it here.   The passages in which
Swift has described and denounced the commercial
system which prevailed in his day are familiar to most
Irish readers.   But we need not refer to Swift, who
was, after all, an Irishman, and may fairly be suspected
of having had some sympathy with his countrymen. I
shall confine myself to English authorities. The names
of the respective authors of the following two quotations will be quite sufficient to negative any suspicion

of an over-statement of the case as against England. In the debate on Orde's commercial propositions, in 1785, Mr. Pitt spoke to this effect :—" He begged them to recollect that from the Revolution to a period within the memory of every man who heard him, the system had been that of debarring Ireland from the enjoyment and use of her own resources—to make the kingdom subservient to the interest and opulence of this country—without suffering her to share in the bounties of nature or the industry of her citizens." The policy was intended to benefit England at the expense of Ireland; but that it did benefit England in the long run is more than doubtful. On this point Mr. Froude observes :—" Ingenuity could not have devised a policy less beneficial to the country in whose interests it was adopted, or better contrived to demoralise the people at whose expense it was pursued. A large and fast-spreading branch of manufacture was destroyed, which was tempting capital and enterprise and an industrious Protestant population into Ireland. A form of industry was swept away which would have furnished employment to the native Irish and brought them under settled habits, which would have made four Ulsters instead of one, and raised each of the four to double the prosperity which the province which preserves the linen trade has, in fact, obtained."*

* The English in Ireland, vol. i. p. 499. For a full account of the provisions of the restrictive laws, see an interesting old work entitled " The Commercial Restraints of Ireland Considered in a series of Letters to a Noble Lord." Dublin, 1779.

If we look into the acts by which this infamous policy was carried into effect, we see plainly enough that English statesmen and English parliaments did not then hold the doctrine that the natural advantages of England and the superiority of the English people were such as to make it certain that, in the matter of manufactures, they would beat Ireland in fair competition. On the contrary, the petitions which led to the Act of 1699, as well as the preamble to the Act itself, go to show that the English manufacturers feared, and had some reason to fear, Irish competition. When we remember the rapid progress which Irish manufactures, and more especially the woollen manufacture, made before the restrictive laws were passed; and when we remember the wonderful struggles which these same manufactures subsequently made to exist and grow, despite of every discouragement, it is not, perhaps, too much to conclude that if Ireland had had fair play from the start, she needed no protection against English competition to enable her to develop a large and prosperous manufacturing industry.

In the fierce agitation which preceded the passage of the Free Trade Act of 1780, the Irish Volunteers hung round the necks of their cannon the famous inscription, " Free Trade or ———." But what they understood by Free Trade was something very different from what the phrase has come to mean now-a-days. " The idea and the term ' Free Trade,' as then understood in Ireland, did not represent what the Political

Economists now call Free Trade. What was sought was a release from those restrictions on Irish trade imposed by an English Parliament and for the profit of the English people. This did not mean that imports and exports should be free of all duty to the State, but only that the fact of import or export itself should not be restrained by foreign laws, and that the duties to be derived from it should be imposed by Ireland's own Parliament, and in the sole interest of Ireland herself."* That this was so is clearly seen from the interpretation which the Volunteers themselves put upon their inscription. " Resolutions were entered into by the volunteer associations in support of home manufactures, *accompanied by a determination to consume no other*."† The so-called Free Trade Act, which was passed early in 1780, as the result of the agitation just referred to, was a tardy concession of a small instalment of justice. Exportation to the colonies and foreign countries, which, in the case of certain classes of goods, had been absolutely prohibited by the previous legislation, was allowed. But the relations between England and Ireland remained the same as before. These relations were briefly as follows :—The importation of English-manufactured goods into Ireland was allowed with some little restriction. There were duties on certain articles, but these duties did not in any case amount to more than ten

* Mitchel's History of Ireland, vol. i., chap. xix.
† Memoirs of Henry Grattan, vol. i., p. 364.

per cent. If there were any exceptions to the last
statement they were so trifling as not to call for
special notice. The importation of various kinds of
Irish-manufactured goods into England was subject
to much higher duties. In the case of the woollen
manufacture in particular the duties were so high as
to amount to prohibition.

The state of things created by the Free Trade Act
remained unchanged for twenty years. In 1782, came
Irish legislative independence. That Ireland advanced
wonderfully in general prosperity during the short
period of her independence is universally admitted.
It would seem that, in spite of every difficulty, the
industries and manufactures of the country shared, to
some extent, in the general prosperity. This was due,
no doubt, in some degree to "the watchful care,
protection, and encouragement given to trade and
manufactures by the Irish Parliament."*   But the
principal cause was probably that referred to by Mr.
Foster in his speech on the Union. "Can those,'
said Mr. Foster, "that hear me now deny that, since
the period of 1782, this country has risen in civilisation, wealth, and manufactures—until interrupted by
the present war—in a greater proportion, and with a
more rapid progress than any other country in Europe,
and much more than it ever did itself before? And
to what has this improvement been owing but to the

* Blackburne on "The Causes of the Decadence of the Industries of
Ireland," p. 47.

spirit, the content and enterprise which a free constitution inspired ?"*

The brief period of Irish independence was closed,
in 1800, by the Act of Union. English statesmen saw
that the time had now come when complete Free
Trade between England and Ireland might be conceded without danger to English manufactures. Pitt
had already, in 1785, attempted to bring about Free
Trade between the two countries by the commercial
propositions of Secretary Orde. It is believed by
competent judges that it was the defeat of the Orde
propositions that first determined Pitt to bring about
a legislative union. I need not here refer to the
means by which the Union was carried : that story,
at all events, has been told often enough. The sixth
article of the Act of Union provided for the carrying
out of the policy which had been unsuccessfully
attempted fifteen years before. Provision was made
for the gradual taking off of all duties upon the importation into either country of the goods of the other.
Some twenty years after the Act of Union, Free Trade
between the two countries was finally established ;
and, as regards the rest of the world, Ireland was
" put on a footing of perfect equality." Had this
been done a century before it was done, there can be
little doubt but that Ireland could have held her own.
But the concession came late. The start gained by

---

* Quoted *id*. p. 48.

England in industrial progress was decisive, and such as rendered it quite impossible for a country situated as Ireland was, to compete with her in open market. The granting of Free Trade between the two countries came also at a time when industrial production was entering upon a new era. Reference has already been made to the report in which Secretary Hamilton, ten years before the passing of the Act of Union, had pointed out to the Americans the crisis through which industry was passing, and the great danger to his country if, at such a time, she allowed herself to be left far behind in the race. The tendency to centralisation in industrial production which Hamilton foresaw was afterwards realised to an extent which probably far exceeded anything he ever thought of. The extended use of labour-saving machinery and the increased facilities of carriage have made it possible for a country like England to constitute herself the workshop not alone of neighbouring countries, but also of the far-distant colonies of Australia.

The result to Ireland of the fatal boon of Free Trade, coming at the time and under the circumstances it did, was such as might have been foreseen. In the last chapter some reference was made to the way in which one application of the principle of *laissez faire*—freedom of contract—has worked in Ireland. We can now see how another application of the same great principle—freedom of trade—has helped to bring about the same results. We are only too familiar with these results. We are but too familiar with land hunger and with famines, with Irish land bills and with emigration from a country already thinly peopled as compared with other countries. These and such as these are the results which could not fail to follow in a country circumstanced as Ireland has been, when once the people were thrown entirely upon the land as their sole means of support. Somewhat similar evils must have arisen in England had it not been for her vast manufacturing industry.

It has been reserved for Ireland to furnish to the world the most signal lesson in history of the consequences to a poor and backward country of establishing a Free Trade with a wealthy and prosperous neighbour far ahead of her in all the requisites of cheap production. With the common theory of the effects which ought to result from such a partnership, we are sufficiently familiar. The poorer country has near at hand a splendid market for her bread-stuffs; she obtains in exchange therefor manufactured goods cheaper than she could produce them herself, and so forth. The real effects of such a partnership are stated by Professor Thompson in language which describes so perfectly what has occurred in the case of England and Ireland, that I shall make no apology for quoting the passage in full. Professor Thompson refers first to what I have termed the common theory : he then proceeds to say :—" But experience shows that just the reverse of this is the case. The rich nation becomes, for a time at least, richer by the exchange; the poor nation permanently poorer. The former, through its command of cheap capital, and by consequence, its greater division and efficiency of labour, can continually undersell the latter in whatever it chooses to export to it ; for it can send in manufactured goods at prices with which the manufacturers of the other cannot compete. The process of accumulating capital in the poorer country is decisively checked; its people are reduced from what variety of industry and mutual exchange of services they possessed to a uniformity of employment in which no man needs or helps his neighbour. Their power of association is destroyed ; money, the instrument of association, is drained out of the country. Nothing is left them but the production of such raw materials as the richer nation chooses to buy, and how unprofitable a commerce of that sort is we have already seen. The country steadily declines in all the elements of productive power, even in the character of the single home industry that is left it. 'From him that hath not' is 'taken away that which he seemeth to have.'"*

"But," it will be said, "*cui bono*, all this discussion about Ireland's past ? Suppose it proved that the absence of manufactures in Ireland is the result of a century of ruinous repression followed by nearly a century of still more ruinous Free Trade, what then ?— What remedy have you to propose ?" I answer that I

* Social Science &c., pp. 234, 235.

have no remedy to propose. I have been endeavouring to show that the case for universal Free Trade
is by no means so clear as English Economists are fond
of assuming. In the course of my argument, I have
instanced the case of Ireland as furnishing a striking
historical proof of the fact that under certain circumstances Free Tree may be ruinous to a country. The
bearing of this historical lesson upon the question of
what is the wisest course for Ireland to pursue under
existing circumstances will be a matter for others to
decide. As already pointed out, the right to protect
home industry in Ireland must stand or fall with the
right to self-government. I am aware that there are
many Irishmen, sincerely anxious for the welfare of
Ireland, who hold that the dream of nationhood to
which the Irish race at home and in distant lands has
clung with such passionate fidelity, is a mischievous
delusion which has seriously impeded, and, until it is
finally given up, must continue to seriously impede the
material progress of their country. I can believe also
that English statesmen may honestly regard this aspira-
tion after nationhood as a mistake ; but I find some difficulty in believing they are sincere when they profess
to regard it as a crime. " A people possessing this
good should surely feel not only a ready sympathy
with the efforts of those who, having lost the good,
strive to regain it, but a profound pity for any degradation resulting from its loss, nay, something more
than pity, when happier nationalities have made victims

of the unfortunate whose memories, nevertheless, are the very fountain to which the persecutors trace their most vaunted blessings."* This much, at all events, seems clear. If this unfortunate country is ever to do any good, we must have either one thing or the other, either legislative independence in some shape or other, or complete and *bonâ fide* incorporation in the United Kingdom. The present miserable system is in name constitutional government, but is in reality personal government of the most odious kind— personal government carried on through the agency and with the aid of Castle officialism, arbitrary arrests, overwhelming forces of soldiers and police terrorising and suppressing every expression of public opinion, and swarms of paid spies, detectives, and informers.† Until this system is swept away, and the question settled one way or the other, there can be little hope for this country. One other thing also seems sufficiently clear. Should the Irish people ultimately decide to give up their dream of nationhood, and to enter into a more intimate union with their ancient enemy, as being at worst a necessary evil, they must also make up their minds to accept for their country the position of a draw-farm for England. If the population of Ireland, already relatively small, were still further diminished, the residue might certainly, under such a system, at-

---

* George Eliot in "Theophrastus Such," c. 18.

† The above passage was written before any signs had appeared of the recent new departure.

tain to a tolerable degree of prosperity.   But that the country would ever develop extensive manufactures or enjoy the advantages of a diversified industry is not to be expected.   Some little good might be done in particular cases by the efforts of individual citizens who might be wealthy enough to afford to lose money for a time, and public-spirited enough to be willing to do so.   But so long as the cheap goods of England have free access to our markets, the growth of an extensive manufacturing industry in this country is a result which, in the natural course of events, cannot take place.

We have now examined the leading arguments by which the advantage of universal Free Trade are commonly supposed to be proved.   We have glanced at the historical evidence bearing upon the controversy in two cases, which are at least as instructive as any we could select.   Speaking for myself, I have no doubt but that Protection is, in certain circumstances, the wise policy for a country to pursue.   But I do not claim to have proved this conclusion in the foregoing remarks.   My object has rather been to show how shallow and foolish is the kind of intolerant dogmatism which English Free Trade politicians are so fond of indulging in.   Strong conviction is a very admirable thing, provided it can render a good account of itself. But I confess I have not much respect for the kind of strong conviction which is obviously arrived at by looking fixedly at one side of the question.   To ridicule and denounce those who differ from you in opinion is often an effective, and sometimes even a justifiable course. But in order that this style of argument may be either justifiable or permanently effective, it is essential that your case should be at least so strong as not to suggest any obvious grounds of doubt. I cannot but think that English Free Traders would do well to recognise the fact that the controversy has long since passed out of the stage at which the advocates of either side can serve their cause by calling their opponents fools, and persons who have no minds to make up.

CHAPTER VI.

Political Economy and Sociology.

" You have founded an entire science of Political Economy upon what you have stated to be the constant instinct of man—the desire to defraud his neighbour."—RUSKIN :—*Fors Clavigera.*

" Philosophy, when we are face to face with real men, is as powerless as over the Iliad or King Lear."—J. A. FROUDE :—*Cæsar : a Sketch.*

IN his essay on the " Present Position and Prospects of Political Economy," Dr. Ingram classifies under four heads his objections to the method of inquiry pursued by the Ricardoan Economists. The four heads are as follows :—(1) The practice of isolating the study of the phenomena of wealth from that of other social phenomena; (2) the viciously abstract character of many of the conceptions of the Current Economy; (3) the undue preponderance of deduction in the processes of research ; and (4) the too absolute way in which the conclusions of the Current Economy are conceived and enunciated. It is obvious that this classification is not a perfect one. The fundamental abstraction of the Current Economy— that which views man as a being actuated solely by the desire of wealth and aversion to labour—might be treated with equal propriety as coming either under the first, or under the second of Dr. Ingram's heads. Dr. Ingram himself admits that his classification is

open to this criticism ; but he thinks that the separa-
tion, although not perfect, will be useful as serving to
" give distinctness and order to the discussion."
Following Dr. Ingram's example, and adopting his
qualification, I would add to his heads of objection the
following two :—(1) The persistent practice of looking at the phenomena of wealth from a strictly cosmopolitan stand-point, and the consequent neglect to
recognise and estimate the existence and effect of
national divisions ; and (2) the habit of catching
at brilliant generalisations, which leads the deductive
Economist to constantly " ignore the fact of the
plurality of causes in the very cases which afford the
most signal examples of it."

In the last chapter certain passages were quoted
tending to show that English Economists not only
admit that in their method of inquiry national distinctions are ignored, but further, that they actually boast
of this as a feature in their method which they have
reason to be proud of.*   Of Adam Smith's great work,
Professor Thompson observes, that " promising to
discuss the ' wealth of *nations*,' it practically ignores
their existence, and treats the whole question as if
there were no such bodies. Smith writes as if the
world were all under one government, with no
boundary lines to restrain the movements of labour
and capital, no inequalities of national civilisation
and industrial status to affect the competition of pro-

* See passages quoted on page 147.

ducer with producer."* In this matter, as in the matter of the want of accurate definition, the charge has much more force as against Ricardo and his followers than as against Adam Smith. If English Economists prefer to elaborate a science of things as, in their view, things ought to be, rather than of things as things are, they have a perfect right to do so ; but they must not be angry, or talk of "ignorant prejudice" if their science, being so constructed, is but little regarded by practical politicians. We have seen that the treatment of the Free Trade question by the deductive Economists is avowedly and strictly cosmopolitan. And we have seen also that, outside of England, the preachings of the Current Economy in favour of Free Trade are but little regarded.

Both the Wages Fund controversy and the Free Trade controversy furnish examples of the tendency of the deductive Economists to catch at crude and hasty generalisations ; and, as already pointed out,† the same may be said of the Ricardoan theory of rent. "The bane of Political Economy has been the haste of its students to possess themselves of a complete and symmetrical system, solving all the problems before it with mathematical certainty and exactness."‡ Speaking of the speculations of Bastiat in the " Harmonies of Political Economy," Professor Cairnes observes :—" He produces, indeed, generalisations

---

* Social Science &c., p. 19.   † See *supra*, pp. 66, 67.
‡ Professor Leslie's Essays &c., p. 241.

which seem to satisfy the needed conditions, but, closely examined, they either collapse into mere identical propositions, or are found to contain some flagrant *petitio principii.*"* The criticism is acute ; but coming from an eminent member of the deductive school, it furnishes a striking illustration of the wisdom of the maxim, that they who live in glass houses should not be the first to throw stones. Again, in another place, Professor Cairnes observes : " It is evident, therefore, that an Economist arguing from the unquestionable facts of man's nature—the desire of wealth and the aversion to labour—and arguing with strict logical accuracy, may yet, if he omits to notice other principles also affecting the question, be landed in conclusions which have no resemblance to existing realities."† Precisely so ; what the student of modern English Political Economy has to complain of is that his teachers are constantly being "landed in conclusions which have no resemblance to existing realities."

The fundamental abstraction upon which English Political Economy may be said to be based is that which views man as a being swayed by two opposing motives—the desire of wealth, and the aversion to labour. Hence it is inferred that in all matters connected with wealth men may be relied on to act in the way which experience tells them is calculated to secure for them the greatest possible amount of wealth

* Some Principles &c., p. 175.   † Character &c., p. 49.

with the least possible amount of labour. Hence again, by an easy and obvious deduction, we are led to the doctrine that the rate of wages and the rate of profit in the different employments of labour and capital are constantly tending to an equality. And thus, when English Economists treat of the causes which determine the rate of wages, what they have in view is the imaginary general or " natural" rate to which, as they allege, all wages are tending, and not the actual rates which exist in various countries and in various employments of labour. To all this the new school of Economists reply that, as a matter of fact, the rates of wages and the rates of profit vary very much not only in different countries but also in the same country. If there be in any sense a "tendency" to equality, it is a tendency of the most abstract and notional kind,—a tendency which is constantly held in check by opposing forces, and which, so far as we can see, will continue to be so held in check for an indefinite time to come. Once convince a French peasant that he can get higher wages for his labour and higher interest on his capital in the Western States of America than in France, and, according to the theory of the Economists, he may be relied on to go to America. As a matter of fact, we all know that, in ninety-nine cases out of a hundred, he may be relied on to stay at home. The desire of obtaining the maximum of wealth at the minimum of labour is as strong with the average French peasant as with most other classes; yet this motive is in his case completely and easily held in check by other motives. This line of criticism is met by the deductive Economists in various ways. So far as I am aware, the ablest statement and defence that has yet been made of 'the method of the Current Economy is that given by Professor Cairnes in his Character and Logical Method of Political Economy.* Professor Cairnes admits that "the desires, passions, and propensities which influence mankind in the pursuit of wealth are almost infinite ;" but he believes that "amongst these there are principles of so marked and paramount a character as both to admit of being ascertained, and when ascertained, to afford the data for determining the most important laws of the production and distribution of wealth, in so far as these laws are affected by mental causes."† According to Professor Cairnes and those who think with him, the method of investigating the phenomena of wealth most likely to lead to useful results is one which may be summarised as follows. The Economist is first to abstract from the intricate net-work of passions and motives which determine the actions of men as they are, one or two fundamental principles which, it is said, are paramount in matters connected with wealth. He is then to reason deductively from these fundamental principles, and to build up a science of human

---

* See in particular Lectures 2, 3, and 4.
† Character &c., p. 41.

conduct upon the assumption that the principles or
motives so abstracted are the only factors which are
effective in determining the result.   Having in this
way elaborated his deductive science, he is then to
introduce the "disturbing influences."   All the passions and motives, other than the desire of wealth
and aversion to labour, which form an essential part
of human nature, and all the social affections which
influence man viewed as a member of a society, are
to be classed together as "disturbing influences."
After these have been duly allowed for, the result may
be taken as indicating with approximate accuracy
the line of action which human beings may be relied
on to pursue.   In a word, the motives which determine human action in all matters concerned with
wealth are to be resolved into a sort of parallelogram
of forces having very unequal sides.   The longer side
will represent the two paramount motives : the shorter
side the disturbing causes, and the resultant will indicate the course which human action,—the outcome of
these forces,—will pursue.   No doubt any method of
investigating the phenomena of wealth which is sanctioned by the authority of thinkers so eminent as Mr.
Mill and Professor Cairnes is entitled to receive, and
is sure to receive, respectful consideration.   One may
be permitted, however, in all humility, to doubt if the
method of inquiry just described can ever lead to any
very useful results.   Up to the present, if we except
a few cases which are plainly exceptional, the prin-

cipal achievement of the Current Economy has been to formulate a series of abstract propositions which are deduced with faultless logic from the premises, but which "have no resemblance to existing realities."

Analogy is not sound argument, but it is often useful in making clear the force of argument. I can find no better analogy in the present case than that suggested by Mr. Ruskin.* The teacher of gymnastics professes to point out the course of action best adapted to develop the physical powers of the human frame. What should we say of the professor of gymnastics who commenced his teaching by stating that he proposed to treat of the human body as being constituted of muscles and flesh without any bones? Upon this assumption an interesting theory might be constructed as to the strange contortions and physical exercises which a man might or should or would perform. The skeleton could then be introduced as a disturbing element. A theory of gymnastics arrived at in this way might be very perfect of its kind, but it would be open to the objection that it would have "no resemblance to existing realities;" or rather, as Mr. Ruskin neatly puts it, it would be "deficient only in applicability." Some people might be simple enough to think that the best course would be to begin by treating of the human frame as it actually exists— flesh, muscles, bones, and all.

* "Unto this Last," pp. 3, 4.

But the method of inquiry advocated by Mr. Mill and Professor Cairnes has at least this merit. It recog-nises the fact that the desire of wealth and the aversion to labour are not the only factors in human nature which influence the result. It recognises the fact that a serious disturbing element exists, and needs, in some way or other, to be taken account of. Other eminent defenders of the deductive school decline to concede even so much. In an article in the Nine-teenth Century for November, 1878, Mr. Lowe,* replying to "some recent attacks on Political Eco-nomy," writes as follows:—"In love, or war, or politics, or religion, it is impossible to foretell how mankind will act; and, therefore, on these subjects it is impos-sible to reason deductively. But once place a man's ear within the ring of pounds, shillings, and pence, and his conduct can be counted on to the greatest nicety. I do not, of course, mean that everybody really acts alike where money or money's worth are concerned; but that the deviations from a line of conduct which can be foreseen and predicted are so slight that they may practically be considered as non-existent." Now this passage would seem to be open to either of two constructions. It may mean (1) that if you place a man in such a position as that the only motives effective in determining his action are motives

* Now Lord Sherbrooke. I retain the name under which the article appears as being that by which the author is best known to most readers.

immediately concerned with the acquisition of wealth, then the line of action which he will pursue is one that can be foreseen, subject to deviations which "are so slight that they may practically be considered as non-existent;" or (2) it may mean that, as things actually are in the world, in all matters concerned with the acquisition of wealth,* men may be relied on to pursue a course that can be foreseen and predicted, no matter what other passions or motives may at the same time be called into play. If the first meaning be the one intended, then I am not concerned to dispute the proposition. So understood it furnishes no answer to the criticisms of the historical school. The point is that, as a matter of fact, men seldom, if ever, are placed in such a position as not to be acted on, directly or indirectly, by motives other than those immediately concerned with the acquisition of wealth. To tell us what men would do in such a state of things is simply beside the mark. The nature of the criticisms which Mr. Lowe is replying to, as well as the explanations

---

* I may here remark that the phrase, "the desire of wealth," is often used in the Current Economy as comprising, in a loose, general sort of way, all the needs, passions, tastes, and aims which the various things comprehended in the word wealth help to satisfy (see Professor Leslie's Essays &c., p. 220). It is obvious that the passion which, at one time and under one state of circumstances, may prompt to the acquisition of wealth, at another time and under other circumstances may have a directly opposite effect. The passion of love will furnish familiar examples.

which accompany the passage quoted, point to the conclusion that it is meant to be understood in the second of the senses just specified.   I will assume that it is so intended.   If this theory of human nature were propounded by an authority less eminent than Mr. Lowe, I should not have thought it deserving of notice. As it is, I hardly know what to say about it.   Assertions of this kind have certain advantages.   They are easily made, and are striking when made in incisive language ; and, even when they are wholly untrue, they are often hard to disprove.

At different ages of the world, and in far-distant countries, there have appeared upon this earth two supreme poets.   In the faculty of seeing into and portraying the passions and motives which really do sway and determine the course of action in this human nature of ours, Homer and Shakespeare " stand alone together far away above mankind."   The Achilles of the Iliad is not by any means a model of Christian perfection, free from or superior to the lower passions of human nature.   He is as covetous and as desirous of wealth as most men ; and all the other leading passions of human nature, good and bad, find their due place in that magnificent manhood.   Every lover of Homer is familiar with the great scene in the ninth book of the Iliad.   A last effort is made to propitiate Achilles.   Agamemnon determines to offer gifts of enormous value—a " priceless compensation."   And the ambassadors chosen to bear the message are worthy of the occasion. The gifts are enumerated, and the appeal is made by one who is such a master of the art of persuasion that his words are described, in the exquisite metaphor of Homer, as being "like to the snow-flakes of winter," which fall softly and produce their effect all the more surely because gradually and imperceptibly. If the ear of Achilles is not in the literal sense placed "within the ring of pounds, shillings, and pence," it is certain that the appeal made to his "desire of wealth" is about as powerful and as artful an appeal as could well be imagined. Here is certainly a fair case to test Mr. Lowe's theory of human nature. If that theory were true, we should expect to find that the priceless gifts would be accepted, and that the great drama of the Wrath would then and there come to an abrupt termination. But this does not seem to have been Homer's view. "Hateful to me as the gates of Hades is he who conceals one thing in his heart and speaks another,"—so says Achilles in beginning his answer to Odysseus. In the spirit of this beginning he proceeds to deliver a reply, which plainly enough comes right from his heart, and in which the complex play of human passion is made to appear with a vividness and a power such that we at once feel that here indeed we are in the presence of a master. In the whole of that wonderful speech there is, perhaps, nothing finer than the lines in which the great chieftain lets his visitors see how vain it is to hope that any conceivable appeal to his covetousness can turn him aside for one moment from the course which he has marked out for himself in obedience to the promptings of outraged pride and outraged love. If there ever was scorn that could be fairly said to wither, it is the scorn with which Achilles rejects the gifts of Agamemnon. Odysseus perceives at once that the answer is conclusive because of its very sincerity and truth to nature. Phœnix, the simple and guileless old man, makes a touching appeal to the affection of Achilles and to the recollections of his childhood. The rough warrior, Ajax, seconds the appeal in his blunt, soldier-like fashion; but Odysseus, the profound student of men,—he who could read the secrets of the human heart,—he sees clearly enough that after *that* speech there is nothing for it but to make his bow and retire.

If from Homer we turn to Shakespeare, we find a refutation of Mr. Lowe's theory, which is, in some respects, even more striking. It would be hard to imagine a specimen of human nature more favourable to Mr. Lowe's view than Shylock in the "Merchant of Venice." Avarice is the ruling passion of this man's nature. Surely of him, if of any man, it might be said that " once place his ear within the ring of pounds, shillings, and pence, and his conduct can be counted on to the greatest nicety." Had Shylock's conduct been determined by the " desire of obtaining the greatest amount of wealth at the least cost of labour," he would have instantly accepted the tender of

Bassanio and cancelled the bond.   Yet here again we know that the master thought otherwise.

> " When I was with him, I have heard him swear
> To Tubal and to Chus, his countrymen,
> That he would rather have Antonio's flesh
> Than twenty times the value of the sum
> That he did owe him."

If I stood alone, I might hesitate to controvert a theory of human nature propounded by so eminent an authority as Mr. Lowe.   But with Homer and Shakespeare on my side I feel more at my ease.

But the objections to the method of the Current Economy do not stop here.   The method which proceeds by abstracting one leading passion or motive of human nature and viewing man as a voluntary machine, acted on solely by the desire of wealth and the aversion to labour, would, as we have seen, be open to grave objections, even if it were true that the desires and passions of men were the only factors determining the result.   But this is by no means the case.   The economic phenomena, like the other phenomena of society, as it exists to-day, are the result of a process of development which has been going on for centuries. The causes which have determined the course of this development are very numerous and very complex. They include causes arising from the circumstances in which man is placed, as well as causes arising from the constitution of human nature itself.   The play of these causes,—their action and reaction,—is almost infinitely complex. So much is admitted even by those who believe in the possibility of creating a complete science of Sociology. To sever the economic aspect of this development from the rest, and examine it by itself, is impossible, and would be useless even if it were possible. All the various phases and aspects of the social aggregate have been developed together. It is obvious enough, for instance, that we cannot have a satisfactory theory of the causes determining the distribution of wealth in a country without first getting a clear understanding of the nature and effects of the system of land tenure which prevails there. This clear understanding can only be got by examining the process by which the system of land tenure was developed. It will hardly be contended that such an examination can be satisfactorily conducted upon the principle of excluding all considerations other than those of a strictly economic nature. "There is, indeed, no more important philosophic theorem than this that the nature of a social fact of any degree of complexity cannot be understood apart from its history."*

It must not be supposed that the fundamental abstraction which I have been criticising is by any means the only mischievous abstraction to be found in the Current Economy. The common definition of wealth is itself an abstraction which, as used by the

* Present Position &c., by Dr. Ingram, p. 21.

deductive economists, has been the cause of much mischief. Abstract Political Economy professes to treat, amongst other things, of the nature of wealth; but of the nature of wealth it really tells us little or nothing. As Professor Leslie points out,[*] the history of wealth—the various forms which wealth has taken at different times and in different countries—is a most interesting and instructive branch of economic inquiry. Of all this the Current Economy knows absolutely nothing. It shelves the whole question with an abstraction, telling us that wealth consists of "all useful and agreeable things which possess exchangeable value."

We may here turn aside for a moment to notice the controversy in reference to the method of Adam Smith. We see a striking testimony to the greatness of Adam Smith in the eagerness with which the advocates of different methods claim him as an authority in their favour. "The Wealth of Nations is entirely deductive," says Mr. Buckle.[†] Mr. Lowe, as we have seen,[‡] claims for Adam Smith the credit of "having founded a deductive and demonstrative science of human actions and conduct." In the article in the Nineteenth Century for November, 1878, already referred to, Mr. Lowe adduces some

---

[*] Essays &c., p. 217 et seq.

[†] History of Civilisation in England, new edition (1873), vol. i., p. 249; and see also vol. iii., p. 309 *et seq.*

[‡] *Supra*, p. 70.

arguments of a rather peculiar kind in support of his view. He seems to be of opinion that a process of reasoning is deductive or inductive according as the general propositions are stated first or last. Because Adam Smith finds it convenient to state his generalisations first, and then to proceed to illustrate and explain by a selection of the more striking particular facts from the observation of which the generalisations have been arrived at, Mr. Lowe concludes that Adam Smith's process of reasoning cannot have been in any sense inductive.* On the other hand, when Professor Bonamy Price advises his brother economists to " retrace their steps back beyond the point at which Ricardo diverged into a wrong path," he seems to imply that the method of Adam Smith is, at all events, radically different from that of Ricardo and his followers. The truth is, that the method of the great Scotchman is neither purely deductive nor purely inductive. It is partly the one and partly the other. The question is discussed very ably and very fairly by Professor Cliffe Leslie in his essay on " The Political Economy of Adam Smith.† " The method of Adam Smith," says Professor Leslie, " though combining throughout a vein of unsound *a priori* speculation, was in a large measure inductive."‡ And again, "there ran through the Political Economy of Adam Smith , . a combination of the experience philosophy

* See Nineteenth Century vol. iv. pp. 865, 866.
† Essays &c. p. 148, *et seq.*   ‡ *Id.* p. 150.

of inductive investigation with *a priori* speculation derived from the nature hypothesis."* The reader who desires to get a fair idea of the merits and defects of Adam Smith's method, cannot do better than read the whole of Professor Leslie's able essay. In concluding this brief reference to the controversy, I will make one further remark. No one can study first the works of Ricardo and his followers and then turn to the "Wealth of Nations" without feeling that he has passed into a new atmosphere. In reading Ricardo you are constantly in the region of abstractions. You see conclusions deduced with faultless logic from abstract premises, and illustrated by hypothetical and imaginary examples. You feel a sort of uneasy consciousness that it is all very well, provided only that the premises tell "the truth, the whole truth, and nothing but the truth." In the "Wealth of Nations," on the other hand, you find yourself constantly in contact with the realities of things. Whether the vast collection of curious facts and observations which make the "Wealth of Nations" one of the most interesting books a man could read, are to be regarded merely as illustrations of truths arrived at deductively, or as specimens of the observed facts from which inductive generalisations have been reached, the result is in one respect the same. Whichever view we adopt the fact remains that the "Wealth of Nations" is a

---

* Essays &c., p. 160, *et seq.*

most interesting book, while the works of the Ricardoan or dry-as-dust school are about as dull reading as a man could have inflicted upon him.

We may now return to the point at which we digressed to notice the controversy about Adam Smith. We have seen that the deductive method of investigating economic problems is open to serious objections. We have noticed briefly the different lines of defence taken up by eminent advocates of the orthodox method. The results arrived at so far may be summarised as follows. The method by which the Current Economy proceeds is first to isolate the phenomena of wealth from the other phenomena of society, and then to investigate the phenomena so isolated by abstracting one or two leading factors and arguing deductively upon the assumption that the factors so abstracted are the only causes which are effective in determining the result. As regards the other factors, according to some authorities, they are to be allowed for afterwards as a " disturbing element ; " according to others they are causes which " may be neglected without perceptible error."* If we exclude a few cases which are plainly exceptional, and in which the purely economic causes are strong enough to outweigh all others, the chief result of this method up to the present has been to formulate a series of abstract propositions which have no resemblance to or bearing upon existing realities ; which are

---

* Mr. Lowe in vol. iv. of Nineteenth Century, p. 864.

deduced with faultless logic from the premises, but which are "deficient only in applicability." There is no rational ground for hoping that the same method will ever produce more useful results. Not that deduction may not have its proper office in economic as in other branches of inquiry. But that, putting out of account the exceptional cases already referred to, the inquiry has not yet reached the stage at which deductive reasoning can be resorted to with advantage. We must first have sound premises upon which to base our reasoning, and these, if they can be reached at all, can only be reached by the method of historical induction. From all which we may conclude that, if a true science of wealth can be constructed at all, it is only by treating it as one branch, if in some respects a special branch, of the wider science of Sociology. Economic phenomena must be investigated in connection with the other phenomena of society, and the method of investigation, for the present at all events, must be historical.

But how much can be done in this way? Is there or can there be a science of society? This question, in various forms, has been much discussed of late years. Is there a science of sociology? Is there a science of history? Is there a science of man? These questions, as they have been handled by the disputants on either side, amount to little more than different ways of stating the same problem. The real question at issue may be stated somewhat as follows :—In how far is it possible from a study of the past to see into and measure the causes which have hitherto determined the course of human history and social development, so as to foresee the course which, under similar influences, the future of humanity may be expected to take, and to operate upon the effective causes in such a way as to secure that the future shall be the best attainable for mankind.

In referring to this controversy, I desire at starting to express my dissent from the views of those advocates of the evolution theory who rely on their law as refuting the Mosaic account of the creation. Human society, as we see it to-day, may or may not be the result of a long evolution from the homogeneous to the heterogeneous. To say that the man who accepts this doctrine thereby impliedly and necessarily rejects the teachings of Christianity, is in effect the same thing as to say that anyone who believes that each individual man living in the world to-day has come to be what he is by a gradual process of growth and development, must necessarily reject the Mosaic account of the creation of man. The law of social evolution, as properly understood, neither contradicts nor supports revelation. It is simply beside the question. It explains, or purports to explain, some of the proximate causes which have made society what it is. It tells us nothing of the First Cause. Every rational believer in Christianity recognises the fact that the Supreme First Cause in which he believes is constantly acting through the medium of secondary or proximate causes, the natural course of which is but seldom disturbed. He need have no fear in accepting the conclusion that amongst these secondary causes is the law of evolution, provided that law be reasonably proved. The great English teacher of the evolution philosophy expressly insists on the fact that of the First Cause we can know nothing. " The reality existing behind all appearances is and must ever be unknown."* That is, of course, unknown by any process of human reason. Anything that we do know of the First Cause must come to us through revelation.

The controversy as to the possibility of a science of history seems to me to be, to some extent, a fight about words. If the disputants on either side would only state definitely what they mean by a science of history, the issue would, I think, be very much narrowed. In the first of his " Short Studies on Great Subjects," Mr. Froude attacks the position of Mr. Buckle. He denies that there can be a science of history, but he shows, at the same time, that by a science of history he means something quite different from what the phrase is intended to convey by those whose views he is combating. Thus he says :—" If it is free to a man to choose what he will do or not do, there is no adequate science of him. If there is a science of him, there is no free choice, and the praise or blame with which we regard one another are impertinent and out

* See Mr. Herbert Spencer's " First Principles," Part I.

of place."* Again, after admitting that "external circumstances have a powerful effect in making men what they are," he proceeds to ask, "are circumstances everything? That is the whole question. A science of history, if it is more than a misleading name, implies that the relation between cause and effect holds in human things, as completely as in all others, that the origin of human actions is not to be looked for in mysterious properties of the mind, but in influences which are palpable and ponderable."† So far as I am aware, no writer of any eminence or authority has ever maintained that there is or can be a science of history in the sense in which the phrase is here explained by Mr. Froude. It would seem, therefore, that the difference of opinion between Mr. Froude and his opponents is, to some extent, a difference as to the proper meaning of the word science. Mr. Froude, I apprehend, would hardly deny that the facts of history may sometimes be made the subject of instructive generalisations. Many such generalisations are to be found in Mr. Froude's own historical writings. Take, for example, the following: "If there be one lesson which history clearly teaches it is this, that free nations cannot govern subject provinces. If they are unable or unwilling to admit their dependencies to share their own constitution, the constitution itself will fall in pieces from mere incompetence for its duties."‡

---

* "Short Studies" &c., vol. i. p. 12.   † *Id.*, p. 12.
‡ "Cæsar: a Sketch," chap. i.

I will ask the reader to observe for a moment the character of this generalisation. Mr. Froude observes that it has more than once occurred in history that certain circumstances, in their main outlines similar, have led to results also alike. Upon this observation he founds the induction that similar circumstances may always be expected to lead to similar results. He does not pretend to analyse the complex network of causes which may have been effective in bringing about the results which he notices. He does not attempt to decide whether factors internal or factors external have been more active, or to estimate in what subtle and complex ways the various classes of factors have acted and reacted upon one another. He takes aggregate results as he finds them ; and he infers that when certain broad, general, facts or circumstances—themselves, it may be, the result of almost infinitely complex causes—have been uniformly attended by certain other general facts or circumstances, we are justified in concluding that, given similar antecedent facts, similar consequent facts may be expected to occur in future. Opinions may differ as to the soundness of the particular generalisation quoted from Mr. Froude. But I apprehend that even the most uncompromising opponent of Mr. Buckle's method of treating history will admit that generalisations of the kind just referred to are possible and useful.

This kind of historical induction opens up a wide field of inquiry for Political Economy : and a field which, so far as English Economists are concerned, has been left unexplored ever since the publication of the "Wealth of Nations," more than one hundred years ago. Induction of the kind here indicated will serve at once to supplement and render more definite the results that can be reached by the peculiar line of historical inquiry which Sir Henry Maine has used with such striking success in investigating questions of Jurisprudence and the history of law. Let the student read first Sir Henry Maine's chapters on the "Early History of Property" and the "Early History of Contract,"* and let him then take up some standard work on deductive Political Economy, and read the chapters in which it is clearly shown that in an imaginary system of perfect freedom of contract and perfectly free circulation of capital and labour, profits and wages *would* tend to an equality. Having done this, he will, I think, be in a position to clearly understand the force of the distinction which I am now dwelling on. Whether any body of doctrine which might result from the system of inquiry here sketched out, would have sufficient particularity and sufficient precision to entitle it to the name of a science, I cannot pretend to say. It is enough for me to know that any system of economic teaching arrived at in the way suggested would be certain to be exceedingly interesting, and could hardly fail to be practically useful.

* "Ancient Law," chaps. viii. and ix.

I have said that the controversy as to the possibility
of a science of history seems to be, to some extent, a
controversy about the meanings of terms.   But I do
not mean to deny that there is something more in the
controversy than a difference of opinion as to the true
meaning of the word science.   Mr. Herbert Spencer,
it is true, does not contend that a science of history
can exist in the sense implied by Mr. Froude in the
passages I have quoted; but it seems certain that Mr.
Spencer's estimate of what can be usefully done in
the way of analysing and explaining the causes which
determine the course of social phenomena differs very
materially from Mr. Froude's.*   In the second chapter of his " Principles of Sociology " he classifies under
two heads the original factors, and under five heads
the secondary or derived factors which determine
social results.   Under each head is comprised a vast
variety of causes; and Mr. Spencer admits that the
action and reaction of these causes and classes of
causes upon one another is almost infinitely complex.
In the first chapter of his Study of Sociology, Mr.
Spencer combats the notion that "prevision of social
phenomena is possible without much study;" but it
seems to me that his arguments go far to show that
"prevision of social phenomena," in the sense in
which he here uses the phrase, is not possible by any

* See, in particular, chaps. ii. and iii. of the Study, and chaps. ii.
and xxvii. of the " Principles of Sociology:" and on the same subject,
see Mr. Buckle's History of Civilisation in England, chaps. 1-5.

amount of study ;* or, at best, is only possible to a very
few rarely-gifted men in each generation. Mr.
Spencer points out and dwells at some length upon
"the incalculable complexity of the influences under
which each individual, and *a fortiori* each society,
develops, lives, and decays." In subsequent chapters
of the same book, he dwells upon the various classes
of difficulties, other than those inherent in the subject
itself, which beset the student of Sociology ; and he
points out the preparatory discipline which the study
demands.† Elsewhere he objects to what he calls the
great-man-theory as an explanation of history. It·
seems to me that Mr. Spencer's conception of the
nature and difficulties of the Social Science is such as
to point to the conclusion that if the government of
men is ever to be carried on upon sound principles, it
can only be by the application in practice of some
form of the great-man-theory. The main object of
good government, we are told, is in the greatest possible degree to conform to, and in the least possible
degree to interfere with the progress of that great
evolution which is the preordained course of social
phenomena. Sociology is the science which points
out how this object is to be attained. But the study
of Sociology is in itself complex in the extreme, is
attended with enormous difficulties, and requires such

* See, in particular pp. 15, 16, and pp. 18, 19 of the 3rd ed. ; and to
a like effect see the " Principles of Sociology," chaps. ii. and xxvii.
† See Study of Sociology, chaps. iv.,-xv.

exceptional faculties as those only can possess who with great natural gifts combine long and patient discipline. Granting these premises, the necessary inference is that only a few men in a generation can attain to that knowledge which is needed for wise government. From all which it would seem to follow that men can never hope to be well and wisely governed until the many who do not see consent to be governed by the few who do. Whether the faculty of seeing how rightly to govern be a faculty of intuitive insight given only to men of genius, or whether it be a faculty which is only to be attained to by such a course of study and discipline as few men can hope to pass through, the result is, in one respect, the same. The teachings of the Lectures on Hero-Worship and the Latter-Day Pamphlets will be true, at all events, to this extent, that the best kind of government will be not government by parliaments and universal suffrage, but government of the many who have not the needful faculty by the few who have.

I have indicated the rough outlines of the method of inquiry by which, I believe, much light may yet be thrown upon social problems in general, and hence upon that particular class of social problems commonly included under the head of Political Economy. Whether so comprehensive and elaborate a science of social causation as that contemplated by Mr. Spencer be or be not possible, is a question upon which I do not feel qualified to express a confident opinion. I have pointed out one serious consequence, which, as it seems to me, would result from allowing the possibility of a science at once so necessary and so difficult. But this does not, of course, in any way render it the less probable that a science of Sociology, as conceived of by Mr. Spencer, does or can exist.

The Current Political Economy has been subjected of late years to some rather severe criticism. English Economists manifest a tendency to take shelter behind the authority of great names, and to regard, or affect to regard, the attacking party with contempt. If the present writer stood alone in attacking their teachings, this line of defence would be very natural and would be pretty sure to be effectual. But the revolt, both in foreign countries and in England, has assumed dimensions which the deductive Economists can no longer afford to ignore. This book is no more than an attempt in some respects to supplement, in others merely to emphasise and drive home criticisms which have the sanction of eminent names. If English Economists can show their method to be the right one, it is high time that they should condescend to do so ; but I would respectfully suggest that, if the defence is to be successful, it must be conducted with arguments very much more convincing than those used by Mr. Lowe in the essay which I have several times had occasion to refer to in the course of this chapter. If English Economists cannot successfully defend their teachings and their method, the sooner they admit the error of their ways and lend the weight of their authority to the new departure, the better will it be for the future of Political Economy.

Printed by M. H. Gill & Son, 50 Upper Sackville street, Dublin.